Jarrold Publishing

CONTENTS

Title page: View from St Peter's

Introducing Rome

'O Rome! my Country! City of the Soul!' exclaimed Byron in *Childe Harold*, and the sentiment may still today serve as an invitation. There are things that are unattractive about Rome, but as a tourist you need bother less with them than with its bright side, which Goethe (another of Rome's passionate admirers) extolled in contrast to the 'grey dreariness' which surrounded him 'back in the north'.

To be sure, you will be unable to avoid at least some of the vexations of a city that has expanded in chaos. A word or two needs to be said on this, and you will know at least roughly what to expect in Rome if you skim through the first few pages of this guide as they come.

First of all, you should think of modern Rome, a city of three and a half million inhabitants, as a 'fertile chaos', and grasp its complexity. It has more contrasts than other big European cities; it is a city with many centres. We find Ancient Rome, Medieval Rome, Renaissance Rome, Baroque Rome and the Rome of modern social, cultural and political life all intermingled. And Rome is also a double capital:

the seat of government of the Italian state (which is often plunged into acute political crisis) and the centre of the Roman Catholic Church, visited by pilgrims from all over the world.

The Roman art of improvising

Rome is not an industrial centre but a centre of consumption. Immigration has ceased. Amid the numerous impressive monuments, there are various signs of decay. The city centre is surrounded by a great concrete belt of rented tower-blocks that pushes out ever further into the Campagna. Yet there is something, the true Roman art of improvising, that keeps this contradictory city together. It is imagination and quick wits rather than order and planning that keep the stream of activity and pleasures going and feed the improvisation. The family (and partly still even the so-called extended family) is the social back-bone of daily economic life in Rome. And most Romans still have some connection with the land, at least retaining deep down in their character the peasant's long-suffering, which enables them to survive difficult situations and to enjoy little pleasures. In general, among these city-dwellers family values are still influential. That is why a stranger feels at once at home: you may sit in the squares, by fountains, on steps peacefully in the sun, and the long summer evenings make it tempting to saunter along the many gaily coloured streets that have now been pedestrianised. A shopping trip becomes a walk through Ancient Rome: you don't have to choose between Art and Life. Lots of smaller streets and squares have literally turned themselves into showrooms, where you may look at clothes or bric-à-brac. In other streets, carpets are laid over the cobbles, and palm- or laurel-pergolas erected, and you can settle yourself down and let the stream of humanity pass you by. The Piazza Navona, the Spanish Steps, the Trevi Fountain, the Piazza Santa Maria in Trastevere: these are some of the places where, amid the Seven Hills, the spirit of Rome, old and new, is palpable.

The more one knows of Rome and its two-and-a-half-thousand-year history, the more deeply one can experience the city. But you will enjoy it even without a lot of homework, trotting through the streets at night in a horse-drawn carriage or enjoying excellent meals at the crowded tables of lively restaurants. There are around seven thousand eating-places in and around Rome, since the Romans' favourite occupation is to eat in company with their friends. And, like so many generations of travellers in the past, from the Pincio or the Janiculum you can admire the famed cupolas and roofscapes, and the serpentine Tiber with the Alban and Sabine hills in the background. Or you can climb the Colosseum and the dome of St Peter's.

City of Seven Hills between the mountains and the sea

Even though the sights of Rome are virtually inexhaustible, you should certainly try to find time for some excursions. In a thirty- to fifty-minute drive you can reach mountains and the sea, wooded hills and lovely lakes, offering scenic, historical and sporting attractions of the most varied kinds.

Besides, Rome's position between mountains and sea ensures a most agreeable climate almost all the year round. The summer is certainly hot, but the sea-breeze, the *ponentino*, brings down the temperature in the evening and at night. Extremes of 38°C (100°F) are rarely exceeded or even reached. Winters are mild. The thermometer hardly ever falls to freezing point. When it actually snows for a few hours,

Rome experiences a virtual state of emergency, since cars and buses cannot climb the Seven Hills. But luckily in a short while the sun gets everything back to normal. The winter rainy season, with its dreadful thunderstorms (there is hardly ever thunder in summer), is punctuated by numerous bright sunny days ideal for walks in the city or in Etruria and the Sabine Hills. In spring it often rains for several weeks starting around Easter, which is an unexpected and nasty disappointment, and the weather then is generally colder and wetter than in winter. Characteristic of the first fortnight in September is the sirocco, an oppressively close wind which causes the visitor to sweat from every pore and makes a holiday quite disagreeable. From the point of view of weather, ideal conditions obtain from May to the middle of July and from the middle of September till the end of November: the days are warm, the nights cooler, and the city is not too full of tourists.

Rome has always adapted itself to foreigners and has profited (and has had to) from this international influx. But the 'industrialisation' of both cultural and religious tourism has brought, here as everywhere else, hazards for the visitor.

Prices have not simply risen, they have rocketed. Services often leave something to be desired, both in hotels and in the utilities: telephones, postal system, public transport. And theft is increasing. But friendliness, helpfulness and openness are the dominant attitudes. If you are cheerful and open, you will generally come off all right. You must be prepared to gamble in the Grand Lottery that Rome is even for its residents: enjoy what it has to offer and don't get ruffled by its various hassles (what the Romans call *contrattempi*).

Before dealing in detail with the different areas of Rome and the city's history, it should be pointed out that of course they cannot in fact be divided up as straightforwardly as is necessary here for the sake of simplicity. On the contrary: Rome is in every sense a variegated city. Ancient Rome is not confined to the famous valley between the Capitol, the Colosseum and the Palatine. You come across bits of Antiquity everywhere, even right beside the ultra-modern Termini Station. And everywhere medieval mingles with Renaissance, Baroque and – unfortunately, so far as the Fascist period is concerned – with modern. The human geography of the city is also variegated: the magnificent palaces have always stood among narrow alleyways inhabited by the poor. Even today rich and poor live cheek by jowl, especially since the redevelopment of the Old City by private speculators has got under way, despite the rent controls imposed on existing tenancies. The luxuriously finished and tranquil upper storeys with their balconies are inhabited by the rich, by ministers and diplomats, and the noisy basements by workers, journeymen and minor officials. Fifty years earlier, it was the other way round: the *bel étage* belonged to the rich, the attics to the poor. There were even philanthropists who left small sums in their wills to all those who could see from their attics (seven flights of steep stone steps) the dome of St Peter's.

Everything is in the process of changing, rapidly if not always for the best. The dome of St Peter's no longer dominates the skyline, nor the ordinary people the streets. But enough of the old social fabric survives for the Old City not to be deserted in the evening and at night as are other city centres. Rather it is a magnetic meeting place, a playground that belongs equally to people of every class and from every part of Italy, far and near.

Essential details in brief

Name:
Roma, capital of Italy and of the province of Lazio.

Foundation:
According to tradition, in 753 BC by the twins Romulus and Remus. In reality, Rome was founded in the 8th c. BC by farmers and shepherds who settled here.

Site:
Rome is on the Tiber (Tevere). There are in the city 25 bridges over the river, some extremely old. Rome is about 25 km from the sea (Mare Tirreno).

Size and population:
The city proper covers 209 sq km, the greater metropolitan area 1,508 sq km. The total population is about 3.5 million.

Language:
Italian.

City districts:
Rome is divided into 22 inner wards (*rioni*), 41 metropolitan districts (*quartieri*) and 6 suburban districts (*borgate*).

Academic and cultural establishments:
Rome possesses two state universities, plus Catholic colleges and numerous institutes, academies and technical colleges; in addition about 70 museums and galleries.

Vatican:
The 'Stato della Città del Vaticano' embraces an area of around 44 hectares, including St Peter's. Over this sovereign state rules Pope John Paul II. Within its territory live around 1,000 citizens of the Vatican City; some 3,600 Italians are employed there. In addition, the Vatican has its own coinage and its own postal system.

Religion:
Christians in Rome belong almost exclusively to the Roman Catholic Church.

Churches:
In the inner city there are around 350 churches; in the metropolitan area as a whole, over 900.

Squares:
In Rome there are more than 300 squares, about 180 fountains and 14 obelisks.

Signposts of history

8th c. BC: The nucleus of Rome develops, a settlement of shepherds on the Palatine.

510 BC: Rome's reliable history begins with the foundation of the Republic. Beginning of the Conflict of the Orders (patricians vs. plebs).

343 BC: Onset of Rome's rise to power in Italy with wars against the Latins and the Samnites.

264–133 BC: Rome begins her conquest of the known world. She occupies Sicily, Spain and modern Tunisia in the Carthaginian Wars, and Greece and parts of modern Turkey in the Macedonian Wars.

133–31 BC: Period of civil war in Rome, which causes the collapse of the Republic.

45 BC: Julius Caesar effectively sole ruler of Rome and her empire (assassinated March 15th 44 BC).

27 BC–AD 476: Roman Empire (Principate and Dominate). Under Augustus (27 BC–AD 14), Rome's cultural golden age. The Empire reaches its greatest territorial extent under Trajan (AD 98–117).

May 11th 330: Byzantium (Constantinople) becomes the imperial capital. In 396 Honorius and Arcadius divide the Empire into two separate parts, Western and Eastern.

476: Deposition of the last Roman emperor.

To 753: Rome ruled by Langobard (Lombard) conquerors.

754, 756: The Donations of Pepin; the Pope becomes the secular lord of Rome and of the Papal States.

Dec. 23rd/24th 800: Charlemagne crowned Emperor by Pope Leo III in (Old) St Peter's.

1305–1420: Avignonese Papacy and the Great Schism. The population of Rome drops to less than 20,000.

16th c: Economic and cultural revival of Rome thanks to exploitation of Church revenues by the popes.

1808–14: Rome occupied by Napoleonic troops.

1870: Rome chosen as capital of the United Kingdom of Italy.

1946: Proclamation of the Italian Republic.

The Appian Way

Phases of history

Origins

Scarcely any town has experienced as many periods and changes as Rome. Its origins are shrouded in myth, in the famous legend of the twins Romulus and Remus – the fruit of the union of a god and a king's daughter – who were suckled by a she-wolf and grew up on the banks of the Tiber. When the two boys became men, they decided to found on this fine patch of land a city, whose fortunes they wished to guide. But too many cooks spoil the broth, and Romulus solved the problem by rapidly getting rid of his brother and declaring himself king.

Historians say that Rome developed from a loose association of shepherds and farmers, who settled on four of the seven hills of future fame. Some time between the 8th and 7th c. BC, they merged together to form a city.

It is certain that the first form of government was a monarchy. But whether there really were seven kings including Romulus is unclear. Some of them however we know by name, for example Servius Tullius, who built the first city walls, about 11 km in length. The last three kings were Etruscans, and the Romans were considerably influenced by the highly developed culture of Etruria.

The Early Republic

Around 500 BC people in Rome evidently got tired of the monarchy. We may assume that a strong aristocratic class had grown up, which succeeded in realising its desire for domination by declaring a republic. Initially this republic was purely patrician, with two consuls at its head. But very soon the plebs too made its claims known and had its interests protected by the tribunes of the people. Serious internal strife by no means hindered Rome's steady expansion: the Romans gradually succeeded in subduing all the Italic peoples who had settled in the different regions of the peninsula. The hardest struggle was against the Samnites in the Apennines, who fought ferociously for their independence. But the Romans' legendary strategic skill was already perceptible at this early juncture: through a series of three wars they succeeded in subduing the valiant Samnites and colonising their cities. By around 240 BC Rome controlled the entire Italian peninsula south of the Arno.

The Carthaginian Wars and the Late Republic

Around the middle of the 3rd c. BC the Romans began to extend their empire beyond the peninsula. In this context, the three Punic (Carthaginian) Wars (264–146 BC) and the wars against Macedonia (212–146) were decisive. Though Rome had to endure a number of reverses, the 'irresistible rise' of the empire began in this period. By the end of the Punic Wars Rome had extended her control round the Mediterranean – much of the Iberian peninsula (by 197 BC), Macedonia (by 148 BC) and Greece (146); in the same year, with the final destruction of Carthage, the province of Africa (modern Tunisia) was established.

The extraordinary wealth that now flowed into Rome from the provinces was reflected in her physical appearance. New districts were built up, the main streets

Left: The Spanish Steps in front of the church of S. Trinità dei Monti

The Ponte Sant'Angelo, built by the Emperor Hadrian in AD 136

paved, numerous temples and two basilicas (law courts) erected. New types of private house, as well as apartment blocks for the poor, began to be built.

But increased wealth also produced sharper conflicts within the political class, the senatorial order. Essentially, the institutions of the Republic were not strong enough to control the ambitions of able generals thrown up by Rome's wars. Sulla emerged as dictator in 82 BC after one round of bloody civil war. Julius Caesar, who had gained fame by conquering Gaul (58–51 BC), defeated Pompey and the other senatorial generals (49–45 BC), and was declared dictator for life in 45. But of course this did not last long: he was assassinated by Brutus and Cassius in March 44.

The Principate

It was Octavian, later *Augustus* ('majestic'), who emerged from the constant civil wars as sole ruler. With him came the shift to the Principate. By then, the city of Rome had half a million inhabitants. During his forty-year reign (27 BC–AD 14), Augustus turned Rome into a capital of magnificent marble, and the emperors who followed him continued this task. A large proportion of the buildings whose remains we can see today belong to these four centuries of the Principate and Dominate, for example the gigantic baths and mausolea, the Colosseum, a large part of the Fora, and basilicas, temples, markets, triumphal arches and columns. By the end of the 2nd c. AD the population had risen to at least a million. Eleven aqueducts ensured a sufficient supply of water; 3,000 people could bathe at the same time in the various bath-houses. In AD 271 the Emperor Aurelian built a city wall enclosing around 1,330 hectares (3,286 acres). Even as the immense empire began to crumble, the building activity in the capital kept steadily on.

Individual Christians were executed in Rome as early as the mid-1st c. BC, and larger-scale persecution continued sporadically, often under popular pressure, culminating in the more serious attempts of Decius (AD 250–51), Valerian (257–59) and Diocletian (303–05) to exterminate the religion. In 311 Christians were granted freedom to worship by Galerius, Licinius and Constantine. Constantine himself professed Christianity: during his reign, the Church was permitted to inherit property and the first Christian basilicas were erected in Rome.

In 330 Constantine caused an open break with the Senate in Rome with his proposal to move the centre of government to Constantinople. Old Rome, which had created the great empire, no longer had any real role as a capital.

Rome in the Dark and Middle Ages

In 396 the Empire was divided into a western and an eastern part. It did not take long for the Western Empire to fall: the Visigoths under Alaric captured the city in 410,

The Colosseum

and further barbarian invasions followed. Hardly anyone in the sorely ravaged former capital took any notice when the last emperor of the Western Empire, Romulus Augustulus, was deposed in Ravenna (476).

The city remained in the hands of the German conquerors into the 8th c., except for a brief period of Byzantine occupation in the 530s. It was the Carolingian victories over Aistulf, king of the Langobards, that first helped the city to a partial recovery (754, 756). Through the Donations of Pepin the popes gained the Papal States, and, with the coronation of Charlemagne in St Peter's in 800, the Holy Roman Empire was formally inaugurated.

Only 25,000 inhabitants remained in the city – scattered groups in a waste of marble rubble. Clergy and nobility struggled fiercely for power, and neglected to defend the city externally. Rome was thus exposed to numerous raids, such as that of the Norman Robert Guiscard, who was accused of having finally destroyed the remains of the ancient city.

The struggles against the nobility meant that, willingly or no, the popes had often to quit Rome. Generally, they retired only a short distance into the Papal States. But

The Victor Emmanuel Monument

in 1305 they abandoned St Peter's throne for Avignon and only returned finally in 1420. Their departure was the ultimate blow, since Rome as a city had depended upon the wealth and patronage of the papacy.

Renaissance and Baroque

With the return of the popes, Rome took on a new lease of life. The Great Schism was settled at the Council of Constance (1417), and Rome was finally declared the seat of the Catholic Church. The Renaissance spirit and the Antique Revival played their part in making Rome once more the centre of interest. Thanks to the popes' readiness to raise loans on the security of benefice income and the sale of offices, undreamed-of new wealth flowed into the city. Every noble family now took pains to provide at least one cardinal or pope and to build at least one palace or villa. An extraordinary building boom began. The greatest architects and artists were called in. In fact the centre of Rome as we now see it dates almost entirely from this period. One outstanding personality was Pope Sixtus V (1585–90), who regulated Rome's road system, laid out squares and public spaces, and had the fallen obelisks dug up and re-erected.

Towards the reunification of Italy

Rome awakened from her political slumber when Napoleon's troops occupied the city in 1808. But the Napoleonic interlude lasted scarcely five years. Another Restoration era followed, under the stolid domination of the Church. Agitation for unity seethed all over Italy, but penetrated Rome only with the election of the tolerant Pope Pius IX. Yet Rome remained the last bastion: Italy was united under King Victor Emmanuel in 1861, but it was only in 1870 that the Italian troops pushed into the city and declared it the capital of the new kingdom. The pope withdrew into the Vatican.

Rome as capital of the kingdom

Its new role produced new problems for Rome which were soon to prove too great for it. There began a feverish immigration from all over Italy. It lasted a century and caused the population to double every thirty years. The immigration was accompanied by an equally feverish and reckless speculative building boom. For the construction of the National Monument on the Piazza Venezia (to Vittorio Emanuele II) between 1885 and 1911, a large slice of the Capitol hill, including the ancient buildings on it, was removed.

The Fascists, who came to power in 1922, continued this monumental building spree. One can view their architectural legacy in the EUR quarter, in the so-called Foro Italico, and in the Via della Conciliazione, the street leading up to St Peter's. The Via della Conciliazione was laid out on the occasion of the Lateran Pact (1929), which was the Italian state's first reconciliation with the papacy it had robbed of its Papal States.

In 1943 the city was bombed by the Allies. Despite this, Rome emerged from the two world wars relatively unscathed. After the fall of Mussolini in 1943, the city was occupied by the Germans for six months. The Allies entered in 1944. The Italian people voted in a referendum against the monarchy and in favour of a republic by a narrow majority of 54.9%. The Republic was proclaimed on June 2nd 1946.

Cityscapes

The cityscapes of Rome are not precisely separated, but overlap one another.

Ancient Rome is centred in the heart of the city. The Capitol gives a view of the Fora straight ahead, and, to the left, of Trajan's Column and Market up to the Torre delle Milizie. The *Imperial Fora* however were partly covered over again by the monumental *Via dei Fori Imperiali*, which leads to the Colosseum. In the depression the other side of the Palatine lies the *Circus Maximus* with the *Forum Boarium* by the riverbank.

Renaissance and Baroque Rome starts, from the Piazza Navona, with the Cancelleria and the Palazzo Farnese, and continues up the Via Giulia; and again from the Piazza del Popolo down the Via del Corso, via the Trevi Fountain to the Piazza Venezia. These two routes take you past innumerable streets, alleys, churches, public spaces and palaces.

Catholic Rome centres on the Vatican City on the other side of the Tiber. The modern area behind the Janiculum (Gianicolo) also belongs to Catholic Rome.

International Rome begins at the Termini Station, thence to the Via Veneto with its big hotels and part of the business quarter. The modern quarter of *Parioli* abuts the gardens of the Villa Borghese; here is the pretty *Palazzetto dello Sport* and Olympic village built for the 1960 Olympics. Beyond the Tiber is the smart Mussolini quarter, the *Foro Italico*, with its Olympic stadium and the residential areas of Vigna Clara and Via della Camilluccia.

Modern Rome in the EUR quarter (the intended site of the Universal Exhibition of 1942) lies half-way to the sea. There are skyscrapers, an artificial lake, modern villas, several ministerial buildings, and conference centres. Express highways run to Ostia Lido and to the popular resort of Castelfusano. Not far away is the airport, *Leonardo da Vinci*, near *Fiumicino*.

Medieval Rome, mingled with examples of the Baroque, starts with S. Maria Maggiore, then continues in one direction to SS. Quattro Coronati, S. Stefano Rotondo, the park of the Villa Celimontana and the Aurelian wall (Porta Metronia), and in the other down the Via Merulana to St John Lateran, S. Croce in Gerusalemme and the Porta Maggiore.

The Rome of the new housing estates includes the bulk of the city. They extend all round and are mostly unenticing to tourists, though full of interest to sociologists.

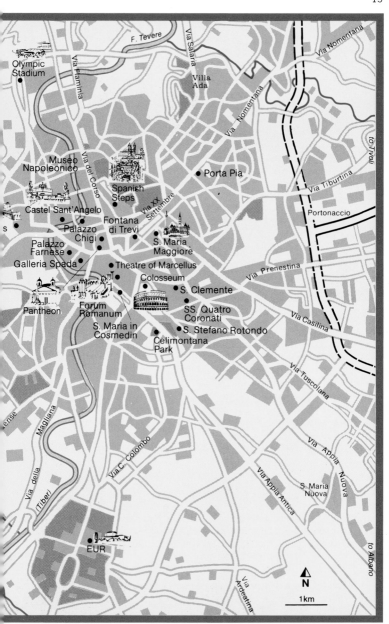

Olympic Stadium

F. Tevere

Via Flaminia

Via Salaria

Via Nomentana

Villa Ada

Via Nomentana

to Tivoli

Museo Napoleonico

Via del Corso

Porta Pia

Via Tiburtina

Portonaccio

Spanish Steps

Castel Sant'Angelo

s

Fontana di Trevi

Via XX Settembre

Palazzo Chigi

S. Maria Maggiore

Palazzo Farnese

Galleria Spada

Theatre of Marcellus

Via Prenestina

Colosseum

Via Casilina

Pantheon

Forum Romanum

S. Clemente

SS. Quatro Coronati

S. Maria in Cosmedin

S. Stefano Rotondo

Celimontana Park

Via Tuscolana

ense

Magliana

Via C. Colombo

Via della (Tiber)

Via Appia Nuova

S. Maria Nuova

Via Appia Antica

EUR

Via Ardeatina

to Albano

N

1km

What Rome has to offer

The following pages put Rome 'on display'. You should make first acquaintance here and briefly review the possibilities so that you may make plans according to your inclination. You will find in the following sections, 'Suggested tours of the city' and 'Rome: a classified directory', the necessary practical help.

Above: The Pantheon
Below: The Forum Romanum

Ancient sites

The Fora

The finest view of the Fora is from the south-east of the Capitol. You need patience and a bit of imagination to decipher the significance that these romantic ruins had in Antiquity. From here were governed not only the metropolis of Rome (over a million inhabitants in the 2nd c. AD) but also the entire empire of about 60 millions, stretching from Africa to Britain. Not far from the famous Forum Romanum with its triumphal arches, temple ruins and sacred rocks lie the other Fora, the Forum of Trajan with its fine Column, the Forum of Caesar and the Forum of Augustus, together with the *Templum Pacis* of Vespasian.

Arch of Constantine

The Colosseum and the Arch of Constantine

The enormous amphitheatre rises right at the far end of the Forum Romanum. In Antiquity it seated 50,000 spectators, and was so ingeniously constructed that the crowd, organised by rank and status, could reach their places in a few minutes. Nowadays you see inside it a maze of corridors and rooms which were once beneath the arena. The corridors for the animals, waiting rooms and theatre machinery were all here. Not far away, at the beginning of Via di S. Giovanni in Laterano, are the remains of the gladiatorial school. On the other side of the Colosseum, in the middle of the road, is the Arch of Constantine, one of the best-preserved remains of Ancient Rome. It was built in AD 315 for Constantine's tenth anniversary as emperor. Only part of the relief decoration was made specially for the arch; the rest comes from earlier buildings. They were ruthlessly sawn to get them to fit.

Via Appia Antica

The most famous of the Roman consular roads led via Capua and Tarentum (Taranto) to Brindisi (in Apulia), where one took ship to journey further east. At its upper end, just outside Rome, the Via Appia was a cemetery. The dead, by law, were only allowed to be buried outside Rome. This part of the city was made into an archaeological zone during the last century. One reaches the Via Appia by the *Porta S. Sebastiano*, which goes through the Aurelian wall. It was built in AD 268 and in good repair until the 19th c.

Pantheon

This vast ancient domed temple (AD 125) is completely preserved and even now there are surely few buildings able to create such a unified and powerful effect. The diameter is equal to the height: 43.2 m. The sole light-source, the circular hole in the centre of the cupola, is 9 m in diameter. The coffered ceiling was once lined with gilded bronze.

Castel Sant'Angelo

Today the Castel Sant'Angelo looks like a medieval fortress. In fact the upper part was simply built above the ancient mausoleum of the Emperor Hadrian. The castle was taken over by the popes in the 10th c. In time of war, they could escape to their fortress through a covered way which linked it to the Vatican palace. The Castel has now been made into an interesting museum where one can see the magnificent papal apartments — and signs of the violent past.

Christian art

For addresses see pages 65–71

Alongside the remains of Antiquity, Rome possesses an inexhaustible treasure of church buildings and Christian art. The most famous, most marvellous and largest complex is the Vatican, which belongs to the Renaissance. But besides the Vatican, Rome still has around 350 churches. Some of them are extremely old, their foundations going back to the Early Christian period, the beginning of which coincides with the Late Antique period. A few examples from the first Christian millennium may be mentioned here.

Catacombs

These originated in the first centuries AD, as a response to the Roman authorities' persecution of Christianity. Here the persecuted Christians buried their dead and built their chapels. The story that the underground labyrinths also served as a hideaway has no basis in fact. The most famous catacombs are at the beginning of the Via Appia; some have very interesting wall-paintings. The catacombs are cut out of the living tufa and in some cases are miles long.

S. Clemente

This church has three 'floors' from three different periods and thus constitutes a first-class museum of art history. The upper church dates from the 11th c. and has mosaics and Cosmati-work to offer. The church below, with frescos of the 9th c., was rediscovered in the last century. One reaches the lowest level, the temple of Mithras (a Roman god), by way of a narrow staircase in the apse.

S. Sabina

This is one of the numerous churches on the quiet Aventine Hill. According to tradition, the church was built in the 5th c. by Peter of Illyria on the site of the house of the Roman matron Sabina. In the Middle Ages it was enlarged and a transept built. The wooden doorway, decorated with carving, dates from the foundation. In the associated monastery St Dominic founded his Order (1216), and met St Francis; St Thomas Aquinas taught here. On certain days the saints' cells are open to the public.

S. Maria in Cosmedin

This incomparable church stands amid ancient buildings in the former *Forum Boarium*. It was built as early as the 4th c. on the ruins of a temple of Hercules. The bell-tower (*campanile*), one of the finest in Rome, dates from the 12th c. There is splendid Cosmati-work on the floor, the lecterns, the bishop's throne and the candelabra. The wooden roof is carried on twenty antique columns. The famous stone mascaron under the portico, the *Bocca della Verità*, which bites the hand of a liar if he puts it into its mouth, was originally nothing but the decorative terminal of an ancient heating apparatus, which puffed hot steam through the openings for eyes, nose and mouth.

SS. Quattro Coronati

From the outside, the church resembles a small fortress. Since its foundation in the 4th c., it has been destroyed and rebuilt several times; its present appearance dates from the 13th c. Inside the 'fortress' is a beautiful marble cloister. Frescos, forecourt and crypt play their part in making a visit very worth while.

S. Maria in Trastevere

This is the oldest church in Rome dedicated to Mary. Pope Julius I supposedly had it built in 340 on the foundations of the oratorium of Callistus, which was believed to be the earliest Christian building. Its present appearance dates from the 12th c., as do the mosaics on the façade, which were probably restored by Cavallini. The apse also has fine mosaics by Cavallini (1291) together with others of varying dates.

Santa Maria in Cosmedin

Renaissance and Baroque

The Renaissance and Baroque styles have stamped themselves on the face of Rome. Between the 16th and 18th c. the popes developed an extraordinary passion for building and thereby gave expression to both their spiritual and their secular power. Many aristocratic Roman families – and many popes and cardinals of the time anyway belonged to such families – also played a part in developing Rome.

Streets and squares

It was probably Pope Sixtus V (1585–90) who altered the appearance of Rome most decisively. He had entire blocks of medieval housing cleared, and built in their place ruler-straight streets which are still characteristic of the city. One example is the *Via Sistina*, which permits a clear view all the way from the *Piazza S. Trinità dei Monti* at the top of the Spanish Steps to the church of *S. Maria Maggiore*. The *Via Babuino*, the *Via del Corso* and the *Via della Ripetta* were added later (all starting from the *Piazza del Popolo*). The *Via Giulia* was part of another grandiose scheme, which was never completed. All these streets are lined with fine Renaissance and Baroque buildings and have for centuries been remarkable for their elegance.

Not the least of Rome's glories are

Piazza Navona

the squares. Perhaps the purest architecturally is that on the *Capitol*, designed by Michelangelo, closely followed by *St Peter's Square* by Bernini. It is pleasanter, though, in the popular squares, which even so leave nothing to be desired as regards architectural beauty. The most famous is the *Piazza Navona*, whose truncated oval shape still indicates the former Circus of Domitian. No less popular is the *Piazza di Spagna* with its magnificent Baroque *Spanish Steps*.

Palaces

Some squares are dominated by large palaces, built by rich Roman families as monuments for themselves. One of the noblest and today the most important is the *Quirinal Palace*, the residence of the Italian president. It was at one time the summer residence of the popes. In summer one can sit and relax in the shade on the stone benches in front of the *Palazzo Farnese*, a heavy, majestic Renaissance building in a beautiful quiet square. Over the Tiber is the *Villa Farnesina* (1508–11), surrounded by a small park, and now a museum of etchings and drawings. The downstairs rooms have all been splendidly restored, except for the Raphael loggia, which is still in progress. Apart from these and other classical Renaissance palaces there is a series of massive and important Baroque palaces, such as the *Palazzo di Montecitorio*, begun by Bernini in 1650, where the Lower House of Parliament (Chamber of Deputies) now meets. Bernini also designed the *Palazzo Barberini*, which is worth looking inside, since it contains a splendid picture gallery. Visible far and wide is the elaborate Baroque tower of the church inside the *Palazzo della Sapienza*, by Borromini.

Statues and paintings

The popes knew how to engage the best artists of all time. But this is not the place to mention the Sistine Chapel or the Raphael saloons in the Vatican Museum. One can find works by Raphael outside museums, in the city's churches, for example in *S. Maria della Pace* and *S. Agostino*. There are works by the passionate artist Caravaggio in *S. Maria del Popolo* and *S. Luigi dei Francesi*. Two world-famous sculptures may also be seen simply by visiting a church: Michelangelo's *Pietà* in *St Peter's*, and his *Moses* in *S. Pietro in Vincoli*.

Statue in St Peter's

The Church today

Church life has gradually lost much of its former festiveness, especially since the Second Vatican Council. Easter Sunday is certainly still the high point of the Catholic year, when a vast crowd gathers in spacious St Peter's Square after Easter Mass to wait for the Pope's Easter blessing *urbi et orbi* from the central balcony. But for years now there have been no flights of doves released nor multi-coloured clouds of balloons, and the crowd's joyful enthusiasm is more subdued. The throng itself is no longer so representative of all the peoples of the world. But it is still striking to see black priests and little Asian nuns, groups of fair-haired northerners and matronly women on tour, old Sicilian or Sardinian peasant families and American tourists all rubbing shoulders with one another. The Sunday before Easter is Palm Sunday, when olive-twigs and crosses skilfully made of twisted palm-leaves are dedicated and then sold.

The other Sundays of the year also attract believers and onlookers, though in smaller numbers. They wait for midday, when the window opens and the Pope gives his usual brief homily, often on some particular Church problem or public issue. The crowd impatiently summon the Pope by blowing their car horns, and when he makes his appearance, and even during the Sunday

The Pope gives his weekly address to listeners in St Peter's Square

St Peter's – centre of the Catholic world

blessing after the short sermon, there is applause, cries of 'Evviva il Papa' ('Long live the Pope'), and renewed loud tooting. This may seem very worldly or even disrespectful, but it is actually a sign of devotion. If a pope is ill, a crowd of people wait anxiously in St Peter's Square. During the last illness of Pope John XXIII in 1963, tens of thousands waited day and night in the square, gazed at the dimly lit window, put little transistor radios to their ears to listen to the latest news and kept quite quiet so as not to disturb the sick Pope. The two fountains were also turned off.

When the Conclave to elect a new pope is in session, Romans and non-Romans gather and wait expectantly for the *fumata bianca*, the white smoke issuing from the little chimney (visible on the wall of the Sistine Chapel beside St Peter's) which announces that a new leader of Roman Catholicism has been chosen: '*habemus papam*' ('we have a pope'). And people wait patiently after

that, full of excitement, to learn the name of the cardinal on whom the choice has fallen.

In 1978, after the death of Paul VI, two new popes were elected. Pope John Paul I died after only thirty-three days in office. His successor, the former Cardinal Karol Wòjtyla, is a Pole – the first non-Italian to 'rule' for 500 years.

Today, the ancient Catholic Church is much criticised, and desire for reform in many areas has grown, not always to the advantage of the institution. The Romans in particular are sceptical or even cynical about the Church. But that is nothing new. The people of Rome, who live so close to the Church's daily life, have always been only superficially Catholic and often outspokenly anticlerical. Yet their whole consciousness is heavily influenced by it. Conservative and tolerant, they have above all a very marked sense of family; intimacy with the Church is part of this sense of family belonging.

A leisurely stroll

In Rome, the leisured onlooker is never alone. Everywhere there are little groups of people just gazing, and not merely in the parks at children playing, or on the Spanish Steps, where young people sit or sprawl in the sun. Romans love looking at other people working. In general, they are always curious about their fellow men.

Take a walk on the *Gianicolo* (Janiculum), the hill south-east of the Vatican, from which one gets the best view out over Rome. On fine days at all times of the year, the Romans love to visit this vantage-point and drink an espresso or aperitif standing at a kiosk.

In summer one can also sit there very comfortably in the shade of the evergreen oaks and eat an ice. From his lofty pedestal, Garibaldi the liberator looks solemnly down on the parti-coloured crowd. By the wide balustrades itinerant pedlars sell souvenirs and *crostini*, balloons and knick-knacks. Along under the oaks there is a little Punch-and-Judy theatre. If you happen to be on the Gianicolo at noon, don't take fright: there is a sudden deafening bang from the gun that announces midday. At one time, when there was less traffic noise, the Romans used to set their watches by the gun's boom. Nowadays, one can only hear it in *Trastevere*.

Oddly enough, people are not dissuaded from sitting and looking even by very loud traffic noise. From morning till night all the tables outside the café on the corner of the very busy *Piazza San Silvestro* are full. The *Via Veneto* however has lost much of its appeal since the long rows of coffee-tables were enclosed behind glass screens. Instead one can now enjoy the gardens of the *Villa Borghese* free from traffic noise; one can sit or lie in the grass, as many do, and gaze up at the tops of the pine-trees, if one happens to be weary after visiting the *Galleria Borghese*, for instance. There is also a small lake where one can go for a row.

The *Pincio* is the Romans' other favourite spot for enjoying the view, and you may be lucky enough to chance upon an open-air concert by the municipal orchestra or the firemen's or police band, which always pulls a crowd. Down below, on the *Piazza del Popolo*, *Rosati* and *Canova*, two cafés opposite one another, compete for custom. There one may see all sorts of odd characters from the film world, and in addition watch the parking attendants, who, for a fee, will squeeze a regular customer's car into a space, or move it from here to there, and continually mollify the martinet police. The parking attendant as saviour in distress is special to Rome, though thanks to the stricter traffic regulations in the centre of town their role is now much reduced.

It is also worth going out to watch on evenings when there is a big reception on the *Capitol*, and the Piazza with the three marvellous palaces is illuminated, for example on April 21st, the anniversary of the legendary foundation of Rome (*Natale di Roma*), or during state visits. The changing of the guard takes place several times a day outside the *Quirinal Palace*, the residence of the president of Italy. You can then look through the portals down the long arcade inside the palace, where the famous *Corazzieri*, the Lifeguards, stand to attention. These guards have to be at least 1.88 m (6 ft 2 in) tall, but are quite often actually 2 m (6 ft 7 in). They look their best in their dress uniforms of white and gold when they appear on horseback at state visits. A thick yard-long horsetail hangs down over their backs from their gilt helmets. When the guardsmen get too old, they usually find new posts as attendants in the Senate, which is in the *Palazzo Madama*.

If you like military parades, you should remember June 2nd, the commemoration of the declaration of the Italian Republic. Apart from the usual units which one can see in other countries, you should note the Bersaglieri who show off their military prowess at the trot, with rooster feathers nodding on their slantwise helmets.

And now back to everyday watching, which happens also to be an important part of the Romans' absolutely favourite pleasure, eating out in as large numbers as possible. Of course no one goes out just for the sake of eating; they go to see and to be seen. One often has the impression that what is really important is the histrionic talent hidden in every Roman, when things really get going at a table, and everyone is talking nineteen to the dozen, roaring with laughter and waving their arms. And it doesn't in the least matter whether the exchanges are clever or banal. Just a few people can easily fill an entire restaurant with merriment: that way they fend off silence, which Romans find quite unbearable. They feel best when surrounded by their fellow men.

The Capitol

Museums and art galleries

For addresses see pages 62–65

The Vatican Museums

The *Vatican Palace* houses in all no fewer than fourteen museums: it is a gigantic fine-arts complex. Here one can see world-famous works of different periods: in the *Museo Pio-Clementino*, for instance, the *Laocoön* (in pre- and post-1942 versions), mentioned by Pliny the Elder as 'of all paintings and sculptures the most worthy of admiration', the so-called *Apollo Belvedere*, and the *Belvedere Torso* said to have been admired by Michelangelo. The three *Stanze* of Raphael (1508–11) are a

The Laocoön statue in the Vatican

must for every visitor to Rome. And those who have visited the *Sistine Chapel* should do so again, since the frescos of Michelangelo, Perugino, Ghirlandaio, Botticelli and the rest have recently been restored and now look quite different.

The Capitoline Museum

This is the oldest public museum of all, created as early as 1471 by the gift of Pope Sixtus IV. It is divided between the two palaces on either side of the *Piazza Campidoglio*. The *Capitoline Wolf*, the symbol of Rome, is to be found here (it has been considered an Etruscan statue; the baby twins were inserted underneath some time before 1509), as well as the *Capitoline Venus*, the *Dying Gaul*, the *Cesi Juno* (thought by Michelangelo to be the 'most beautiful object in Rome'), the little bronze *Spinario* (in the Early Renaissance, one of the most famous Antique sculptures), and the *Apollo* that was Shelley's favourite sculpture. On the first floor of the *Palazzo dei Conservatori* is the *Sala degli Orazi e Curiazi*, the council chamber of the Municipal Government of Rome.

Villa Giulia

This lovely Renaissance villa (the country villa of Pope Julius III) houses the biggest and most comprehensive collection of Etruscan art. Nowhere else in the world is there such an opportunity to acquaint oneself with the remains of the highly developed Etruscan civilisation.

*Right: The Sistine Chapel:
fresco by Michelangelo*

Museo della Civiltà Romana (EUR)

At first you will be taken aback: not a single item in this museum of sixty rooms is original. But you soon appreciate that the different aspects of Ancient Rome can be studied much better in reconstructions and models, for example town planning, craft industries, agriculture, medicine, law, religion. The prize exhibit is the model (200 sq m) of the city of Rome in the 4th c. AD.

Curiosities

Among Rome's museums are a number of curiosities which for those with a sense of humour are well worth a visit. One thinks of the *Museo Francescano* of the Capuchins in the Via Veneto, whose crypt is decoratively arranged with the skulls and bones of former friars; of the *Museo Napoleonico* in the Via Zanardelli, where Napoleon's personal effects are on view; the *Nativity Crib* museum (open all the year round); or the *Museo della Criminologia* in the Via Gonfalone, where you can study the arts of the criminal past and present.

Art galleries

Rome possesses a whole series of painting galleries, such as the *Galleria Borghese*, the *Galleria Barberini* and the *Galleria Spada*. They are mostly in the palaces of the old aristocratic families of Italy, since most are based on the former private collections of these families.

Modern Rome

If you wish to see modern Rome you must take the Metro from the Termini station or one of the numerous buses that go along the Via Cristoforo Colombo to EUR, which is on the way to the sea. EUR is an abbreviation of *Esposizione Universale Roma* and replaces the former name *E42* (Mussolini intended to hold a universal exhibition there in 1942). Several typical fascist buildings had already been built (the team was directed by Marcello Piacentini, Italy's most prominent inter-war architect) by the time Italy entered the war; at its end the half-completed exhibition site lay deserted. The land, some 430 hectares, belonged to the State, which wished to clear it. Without the State or the municipality contributing a penny, Professor Testa, the Commissioner of the EUR Corporation, developed EUR as a monumental complex. Over half its area is open space. An 'environment-friendly' central plant supplies the entire quarter with hot water. For the Olympic Games in 1960 various arenas were designed by the best Italian architects (Nervi and his pupils): the *Palazzo dello Sport*, *Motovelodromo*, *Velodromo* and *Piscina delle Rose*. Nowadays skyscrapers tower round the 400-m-long artificial lake, among them the ENI (the State oil and natural gas company) building, with its glass curtain-wall. A number of ministries have moved to EUR as has the Christian Democratic Party (PDC). The modern villas and parks are also worth seeing.

The most important goal for anyone with cultural interests is the *Museo della Civiltà Romana*. It gives via models a unique panorama of the history of the Roman Empire, reconstructions of ancient buildings, and plaster-casts of the reliefs on Trajan's Column.

Parioli and Monte Mario

Lots of foreigners live in Parioli. This is one of the better places to live, from where one can get quickly into the centre. Nowadays it is so heavily built over that one could get claustrophobia, but it still counts as a 'good address' – for burglars too, who frequently make it their target. So you should not be surprised that in many *palazzi* (blocks of flats) a sour caretaker keeps a sharp look-out. The name Parioli is derived from the Latin *paries*, 'wall'; a wall once surrounded low-lying properties at the nearby *Ponte Milvio*. Several good restaurants have recently grown up in Parioli, including *Celestina*, where one can find excellent beef, and *Il Caminetto*, which has a really pleasant atmosphere – and hence is always crowded. Other favourite places for foreigners to live are *Vigna Clara*, the highest part of Monte Mario (where the Hilton Hotel is), *Viale Cortina d'Ampezzo*, *Via della Camilluccia* and *Via Fleming*. Every foreigner who settles in Rome will if possible get 'up and out', to a penthouse on one of the numerous hills outside, from where the dome of St Peter's is visible.

Porta Pia

A propos Porta Pia, a short lesson in Italian history is called for. The inner façade of the Porta Pia itself was

Opposite: Palazzo della Civiltà del Lavoro, EUR

designed (c. 1561) by Michelangelo for the (Milan) Medici Pope Pius IV. Inside it however is the *Museo Storico dei Bersaglieri*, and on the opposite side of the city wall there stands a dramatic monument (currently invisible, as it is being restored) to the Bersaglieri troops who in 1870 made the historic breach in the wall at this point and after a brief struggle forced their way into the city, which was all that remained of the Papal State. That was September 20th 1870: hence the name of the street that leads up there, the Via XX Settembre. The Italian army lost five officers and forty-three men, the papal troops sixteen. The festival commemorating September 20th was abolished when in 1929 Mussolini signed the Lateran Pact in the Lateran Palace and thus sealed the reconciliation between Church and State.

Local colour

Pifferi

In the period leading up to Christmas the *pifferi* and *zampognari* turn up in Rome. These are the shawm-players and bagpipers from the little hill-towns of the *Ciociaria*, around Anagni. They wear traditional shepherds' dress: long fleece waistcoats, black knee-breeches and *ciocie* (hence the name of the area they come from), sandals consisting of leather soles and lacing thongs. Their legs are thickly wrapped up to the knee with strips of white linen. Many have no musical ability at all: you can tell from the thin notes they wring from their bagpipes and the way they forthwith hold their hats under your nose for money. But there are also some real musicians who play with great skill and verve.

Chestnut-roasters

Some years ago a newspaper campaign luckily succeeded in preventing the municipal authorities from banning the chestnut-roasters. The idea was that they were a blot on the Roman landscape. Many immigrants from the poorest quarters of Rome earn their living in the winter months from *caldarrosti* (roast chestnuts). They sit at street corners and in front of cinemas by their primitive charcoal ovens with grill and copper lid – mostly older men, but also teenage boys or women with children. With inflation now, you usually get about ten hot chestnuts for 1,000 lire.

Pedlars

The Ancient Romans are known to have nibbled what modern strollers buy from the pedlars at street corners, in squares and parks: lupin seeds, pumpkin seeds, olives in brine, raisins and dried plums. Later additions were peanuts (*noccioline americane*) and *popcorn*. In cheap cinemas, in Trastevere or the suburbs, the floor is covered with pumpkin-seed shells and olive-stones just as the Colosseum was 2,000 years ago.

Fountains and water

In the streets and open spaces of Rome there are altogether 180 fountains and 1,400 drinking fountains. The great aqueducts, some of which have carried water from outside the city since

Chestnut-roaster

ancient times, all have a *mostra d'ac-qua*, a great formal fountain, at the end. The *Fontana di Trevi* is the culmination, so to speak, of the *Acqua Vergine*, and the Fountain of the Naiads in the Piazza Esedra near the Termini station that of the *Acqua Marcia*. The *Acqua Felice* comes out at the Fountain of Moses near the Grand Hotel on the Piazza San Bernardo. The *Fontanone* on the Gian-icolo is the magnificent 'moated castle' of the *Acqua Paola*. And the great new aqueduct, the *Acqua del Peschiera*, has acquired at least a jet — albeit an unimaginative modern one — in the fountain on the *Piazza degli Eroi* at the bottom of the Monte Mario.

Buskers

In many Roman restaurants, especially in Trastevere, buskers come to the table while you are eating; they play the accordion and the guitar and there is often a vocalist as well. Buskers are generally a nuisance, since one can only get rid of them either by energetic shak-ing of the head and shooing gestures or by giving them a 1,000-lire note immedi-ately. But in the case of buskers with a good opinion of their prowess, the latter course has the undesirable conse-quence that the lady of the party gets an encore direct in her ear.

Their songs no longer have any con-nection with Roman traditional culture. It is just as well if one does not quite understand the words, which are often risqué. Most musicians have anyway already shifted to straightforward senti-mentality. The best-known such songs are 'Arrivederci Roma...' (Farewell, Rome...) and 'Roma non far la stupida sta sera...' (Don't act stupid tonight, Rome...). There are also flower-sellers who work the restaurants and will offer you single roses (also for 1,000 lire). Beggars are generally made scarce by

Vendor of lottery tickets

the waiters. The itinerant sellers of cheap (stolen) cigarettes are tolerated until the clientèle have bought what they want.

Popular tradition in Rome

This unfolds constantly, not just during the *Festa di Noantri* in the last week of July in Trastevere, but every evening – in the *Piazza Navona*, the *Piazza S. Maria in Trastevere*, the square in front of the *Trevi Fountain* and so on. In the *Castelli Romani* (the Alban Hills, Frascati, Grot-taferrata, Monteporzio, etc.), you may come across a Roman wedding break-fast, with eighty people celebrating in a specially decorated restaurant garden – a spectacle in itself. They even drink the health of strangers, and you need only raise your glass, laugh and wave. That brings luck, for the spectator too!

Social life

See also page 77

Modern cultural life in Rome is lively, but you need to be initiated. People meet in the bookshops (*Feltrinelli* in the Via del Babuino) and listen to stimulating talk of new books so they can then go, if invited, to one of the Roman literary salons. For foreigners, there is the opera (not the best in Italy), and one or two theatres (*Teatro Valle, Teatro Quirino*), where Giorgio Strehler (director of the Piccolo Theatre, Milan, since 1947) and Franco Zeffirelli have directed plays. The new theatre culture (basement-theatre) of the young avant-garde is popular, but you can only form an opinion if you are fluent in Italian and au fait with current issues.

In summer, everything is for tourists: open-air performances in the *Baths of Caracalla*, in *Ostia Antica*, in the little Roman theatre by *Tasso's Oak* on the Gianicolo. There is also an open-air theatre for true Romans, the *Villa Aldobran-dini*, high above the Via Nazionale, in an old Roman garden. The Ensemble Durante puts on Roman farces there. A real delight, even if you don't understand Italian, since actors and audience are mingled together.

Nightspots are called *Nights* in Rome, from which you may conclude immediately that they only came in after the War. They generally have a difficult time, since the average Roman is a real family person and spends most evenings at home. Nevertheless there are some places for foreigners and for the flash set to go. That does mean of course that you have to fork out rather a lot if you want to have a good dance or evening out, unless you entrust yourself to one of the buses of *Rome by night*, where you can take your pick of prices (*Univers, Appian Line, Cook, American Express, CIT*). Probably the easiest and cheapest way of seeing a bit of Roman nightlife is to take such a trip and be

St Peter's Square

dropped off here and there for a drink. Of course, this way you would just be one of a group of foreigners.

A few of the best-known nightspots may be listed, without any guarantee that they can still be found under the same name and in the same location. The poshest nightclub is in the basement of the well-known restaurant *Hosteria dell'Orso*, but called *Blue Bar*, 25 Via dei Soldati; it is in Rome's oldest 'hostelry', where Rabelais put up in 1580. There is also *Club 84* at 84 Via Emilia, *Capriccio* at 38 Via Liguria, and a group of others around the Via Veneto. *Gattopardo*, 97 Via Mario de' Fiori, is a gigantic nightclub and not expensive. *Scarabocchio*, Piazzetta dei Ponziani, was one of the first to replace the musicians with stereo and a disc-jockey. The *Bar della Pace* in the street of the same name is really snug: good news for people who like things sentimental.

To enjoy yourself properly, you must be not merely with real Romans, but with the regulars of a restaurant. Anyone who first eats in the *Ulpia* in Trajan's Forum and then goes on to dance in the *Taverne* can hardly do better.

Roman society

You can glimpse Roman high society, at least from afar, at the horse races in the *Piazza di Siena* (Borghese gardens) in May (they are on for a fortnight). The pillars of Roman aristocratic society are the Torlonia, the Odescalchi, the Borghese, the Barberini, the Pallavicini, the Chigi and the Ruspoli. They also have their clubs, which are extremely difficult to get into, for example *Gli Scacchi* (Chess Club), 4 Piazza S. Lorenzo in Lucina, where in fact chess is hardly ever played (and politics are never mentioned). It has an excellent restaurant, and the main topic of conversation is horses. You are even less likely to be

admitted to another club, *La Caccia*, 19 Largo Fontanella Borghese. For that reason, no exact report can be made of how the élite pass their time there, except to say that lots of people have been expelled because their views were not quite the accepted ones. It is clear from the names of the two clubs *Il Golf* (3 Via dell'Acquasanta) and *Golf Club* (195 Via Cassia) that the élite assemble there for a particular purpose: playing golf. Anyone willing to pay the stiff membership fee may join, so long as he is a member of an old aristocratic family, the 'film aristocracy' or the 'in' set!

In Rome as elsewhere, horses are also part of high society. Before the turn of the century, fox-hunting in the Campagna was a sport of the élite, who were thus very much out of place in the environs of Rome at that time. Nowadays one joins the *Società Romana della Caccia alla Volpe*, whose headquarters are at 55 Via del Pozzo delle Cornacchie. But the middle, and even the lower-middle, classes have now got involved on a wider basis with horses. You can simply learn to ride, by joining the *Società Ippica Romana*, Via Monti della Farnesina, or by going along to the riding school of the *Fratelli d'Angelo*, 871 Via Flaminia. The posh garden suburb *Olgiata*, 19 km from Rome on the *Via Cassia*, has its *Centro Ippico Olgiata*, with a large spread of land.

Since the tourist is usually not in a position to attend an exclusive reception, one or two places where one may come across high society may just be mentioned. *Baretto*, the dim little bar in the Via Condotti, is a favourite place to drink aperitifs, and *Zi' Rosa*, in the Via della Ripetta, a smart place to eat. It's also the done thing to go to *Number One*, a nightspot at 2 Via Lucullo, a place much loved by princelings and the 'money aristocracy'.

Eating and drinking

Roman cookery

One can say in general that Roman cooking is nowadays very mixed, just as the population is a mixture of immigrants from every province. Rome is a melting-pot in every sense.

Hardly anyone could like real traditional Roman cookery, since the Romans were originally poor. They made a virtue out of necessity, in that they made their finest dishes from the cheapest bits of meat, the innards, and from the cheapest vegetables, herbs from the meadows. But this sort of food is disappearing, in step with poverty and industriousness. Who today would go looking for herbs or gathering snails and frogs? Who still cooks calf innards that have to be washed a dozen times? If you tour round the Campagna, in small villages, in the grubbiest-looking eating places, where there is only a piece of paper on the table instead of a table-cloth, you can still come across this simple fare (and find home-made wine). But you have to create such chances yourself. To name names would do harm, since as soon as a place to eat is known, the quality plummets.

Eating habits

If you do not have to take breakfast in your hotel because it is included in the price, it is sensible to eat it in a 'stand-up' bar. The coffee (*espresso*, which doesn't mean top-speed but made 'expressly' for each customer) is everywhere excellent, whether you order it black (*normale*) or *macchiato* (with a dash of milk) or *latte macchiato* (milk with a dash of coffee). In addition every bar keeps fresh rolls (*cornetti*), often still warm, or other kinds of *brioches* too numerous to mention. You may of course repeat this espresso-breakfast several times during the morning. There are Romans who consume a dozen *espressi* and, especially when it is hot, are none the worse for it.

Lunch

What you do for lunch naturally depends on the time of year and your timetable. The Romans generally take it seriously, as with everything to do with eating and drinking. But the altered office-hours (banks and many offices no longer take a three-hour break at midday) mean that the *rosticcerie* too are nowadays very popular. These are fast-food shops, where one can eat standing or sitting. You generally get a complete meal, with spaghetti course, main course (meat and vegetables) and afterwards cheese or fruit. Even in crowded *rosticcerie*, the service is individual: the waiters may arrive in a lather but they never lose patience. Romans would find that really insulting. If you eat lunch in an ordinary restaurant, you are assumed to be a normal diner, that is, you want all three courses. That you only want a plate of spaghetti is simply incomprehensible to the waiter. If you don't want to eat any more, point to your stomach and make a wry face: he will grasp that in a trice and feel dreadfully sorry for you.

Dinner

Dinner is of course the high spot of the day. Anyone who has no time (or no room) for it will simply be thought

A café in the Piazza Navona

extraordinary. The Romans only drink wine with meals. At the end of the *cena* (dinner), however, they finish the meal off with a small glass of liqueur or *eau-de-vie*. Depending on the restaurant and on how much you have eaten, this is frequently offered *gratis* by the owner. You accept with a friendly grin of thanks: what an agreeable survival of the ancient hospitality code!

If late in the evening people still want to enjoy the cool air in some Roman square, they generally order an ice. But whisky is also now at home in the Italian metropolis.

Water

All round Rome there are numerous mineral-water springs, though nowadays they are mostly tapped commercially. The custom has grown up for a bottle of mineral water to be put on the table in most eating places, generally unrequested. Many people don't dare to refuse it for fear of appearing mean. The true Roman however will have none of it: for him, wine is enough or, if need be, *acqua naturale*, water from the tap. The water in Rome is generally fresh and good, except in old houses in which it comes from a tank in the attic and is thus lukewarm in summer.

Tipping

It is usual, apart from the percentage normally included in the price, to leave a further 5% tip. Even the owners of eating places are not offended when one leaves a tip on the table. Such places are obliged to make out a bill with a tax number but they do not always do so. You should ask for one, since you could be required to produce it if the restaurant is officially inspected.

Good restaurants

For addresses see pages 75–76

Alfredo all'Augusteo, 30 Piazza Augusto Imperatore, tel. 678 1072, is among the most famous gourmet restaurants in Rome. An unresolved debate rages over which Alfredo is actually the real Alfredo, since there is another in the nearby Via della Scrofa, in the same building where Alfredo the master chef had his first restaurant. At any rate, one can eat very well in either, on account of the competition between them. The basis of this fame is the *fettuccine all' Alfredo*, home-made fettuccine with lots of butter and rich Parmesan, all mixed together – and this is the important bit – by Alfredo himself with lightning speed and golden cutlery. Another ceremony is setting fire to the *crêpes suzettes* (*frittate*) for the sweet course.

La Capricciosa, 8 Largo dei Lombardi, tel. 687 8636, is also in the centre and offers a wide range of gourmet dishes, with the added advantage of having a pizzeria on the premises. This restaurant is a favourite with refined Romans who do not mind spending a bit on eating and drinking, and want to ensure that the waiter will do that little bit extra if demanded. You may sit outside.

Otello alla Concordia, 81 Via della Croce, tel. 679 1179, is a busy restaurant of medium quality and price. It is especially agreeable in summer to sit in the courtyard pergola near the plashing fountain, above which fresh vegetables and fruits are built up into a sort of altar.

Lots of artists, lots of young people, quick and extremely attentive service.

Dal Bolognese, 1 Piazza del Popolo, tel. 361 1426. In this case you really must book beforehand by telephone, because this excellent restaurant is much patronised by Roman high society. It practically rubs shoulders with the *Caffè Rosati*, where the smart set drinks aperitifs, and is opposite the *Caffè Canova*, where intellectuals have their rendezvous. The basis of the menu is, as the name suggests, still bolognese, with international additions, especially as regards the drinks list.

Carmelo alla Rosetta, 9 Via della Rosetta, tel. 656 1002, is not far from the Pantheon and has the reputation of being one of the best fish restaurants in Rome. As the Romans are passionate fish-eaters, the restaurant is notoriously crowded: you sit elbow to elbow and conversation is occasionally made difficult. But the atmosphere is lively and the service superb.

La Fontanella, 86 Piazza Fontanella Borghese, tel. 678 3849, is famous for its marvellous Tuscan dishes and fine Chiantis. Since the service is good and brisk, you can often see large parties there having a real feast. These are mostly office groups, putting the weekly grind behind them with the classless good fellowship of the table.

Nino, 11 Via Borgognona, tel. 679 5676, is ideal when the weather is not so good: near the Spanish Steps; well looked after; not too big; the best sort of business clientèle; offering a number of excellent specialities of the house (such as *fagioli al fiasco*, pickled beans); well-kept carafe wine; moderate prices.

Al 34, 34 Via Mario de' Fiori, tel. 679 5091. A small, cosy, family-run restaurant in the centre of town, with the particular advantage of not being expensive. It is famous not only for its fettuccine dish with mushroom sauce and its *boeuf aux herbes*, but also for its sweet dishes, prepared with particular affection by the Neapolitan chef.

Cannavota, Piazza S. Giovanni in Laterano, tel. 77 5007. Good Italian cooking in the shadow of the immense bulk of the Lateran church. Extremely agreeable prices. Take note of the unusual pasta dishes and sample the *Scampi alla Cannavota*.

Checchino, 30 Via di Monte Testaccio, tel. 574 6318, is built into a cavern in the Monte Testaccio, the Ancient Roman rubbish heap made of broken amphora sherds. The site itself is worth seeing – and if you arrive early enough, do visit the Protestant cemetery just by the *Pyramid of Cestius*, where Keats and Shelley, and many other notable people, are buried. At Checchino's you get typical Roman food, i.e. lots of sheep and calf offal prepared in traditional ways. You could hardly find a better example of true Roman cookery!

Il Buco, 8 Via S. Ignazio, tel. 679 3298, is another Tuscan restaurant, which merely means that the Florentines have done much to enrich Roman cookery. Recommended here is the plate-sized *bistecca fiorentina*, the best means of recuperation after a hard day's sightseeing.

Papa Giovanni, 4 Via dei Sedari, tel. 656 5308. Eating in this restaurant is not exactly a cheap pleasure, but it is worth it, for it is one of the best not merely in Rome but in the whole of Italy. The menu of Papa Giovanni keeps strictly to what is currently in season: its marvellous creations are ravishing.

Self-service restaurants: Tavola calda

If you want to eat really cheaply, go to one of the numerous *tavole calde*. Because the Romans have largely given up their long midday break, this practical and cheap way of eating has become common in recent years. If you are in a hurry, you eat standing up, but you may also sit at your ease. The following offer a wide choice of hot and cold food: *Il Delfino*, 67 Corso Vittorio Emanuele; *Canova*, Piazza del Popolo; *Piccadilly*, 2 Via Barberini; *Doney*, 145 Via Veneto.

Alfresco meal in the Piazza Navona

One or two highlights

The Ponte Sant'Angelo still has three original ancient arches (AD 136) beneath the Baroque cladding and additions.

Porta Portese, the famous second-hand market (Sunday mornings only), takes its name from the former city gate which led via the *Via Portuense* to the harbour (*Porto*). The gate was later rebuilt by the popes. At the end of the War a barter-market grew up, which has since enlarged itself into a flea-market extending for well over a mile. Nowa-days it is only worth the while of real experts and enthusiasts to hunt for bargain antiques. Warning: the card-players, mostly in groups with one eye out for the police, are out-and-out sharpers!

Where the **Via Gregoriana** meets the *Via Sistina* one can see the balcony of the house belonging to Henriette Hertz, who more than a hundred years ago made the building and library into a German research foundation for the study of medieval and Renaissance Rome. Today the *Biblioteca Hertziana*

The Ponte Sant'Angelo, leading to the Castel Sant'Angelo

also incorporates the surrounding *palazzi*. Moreover, so many famous people have lived in the *Via Gregoriana* that practically every house has to carry a memorial plaque: Salvator Rosa, Poussin, Johann Friedrich Overbeck, Angelica Kauffmann (whose studio Goethe often visited), and Gabriele d'Annunzio. Ferdinand Gregorovius, the great German historian (1821–91), who wrote his *History of Rome in the Middle Ages* here, valued the street's rural tranquillity, and rightly feared that once the Piedmontese got into the city of the popes the 'new, pushy ways' would prevail.

Piazza di Spagna: 159 steps lead up from the *Barcaccia*, Bernini's fountain, to the church of *S. Trinità dei Monti*. At one time the Piazza and steps formed a sort of no-man's-land, where the papal police turned a blind eye when the foreign artists got drunk and boisterous – the same forbearance as is now shown the young people who often spend the night on the steps during the high summer and have nowhere to wash in the morning but Bernini's fountain. It might then have been a sense of tradition which induced McDonald's to install their first Roman hamburger outlet in the neighbouring Piazza Mignanelli in 1986, an event which so aggrieved the intelligentsia that they organised a solemn protest against the pollution of the Roman way of life.

Via Margutta still has a reputation as the artists' quarter, though nowadays

perhaps more rich foreigners like to treasure (and pay for) the studios and roof-gardens below the belvedere of the Pincio. There are still plenty of art studios and craft workshops, but only amateurs and frightful kitsch-artists display their work at the biannual (spring and autumn) street show, *Mostra di Via Margutta.*

Via Veneto (properly *Via Vittorio Veneto*) is now a shadow of its former glory. Hardly any trace remains of the 'dolce vita' of Fellini's famous film. The old coffee-houses have changed owners and been hideously 'modernised'. The long rows of tables on either pavement in front of the shops and hotels have been 'protected' by ridiculous glass verandahs. Only tourists who don't know any better make their pilgrimage here, to find at best by day a few expensive shops and later on a sleazy, lacklustre nightlife. There are, though, the two great newspaper kiosks that day and night carry vast quantities of papers and periodicals in every language. At the lower end of the Via Veneto, near the Piazza Barberini, is the church of the Capuchin Friars (S. Maria della Concezione) in whose crypt you can see the artistically arranged bones of 4,000 Capuchins (enjoyably creepy!).

Via Sistina, named after Sixtus V, who laid out the street in the 16th c., was once the Pall Mall of Rome. Nowadays it is lined with fashionable clothes boutiques that cater for the guests of the high-class hotels.

Campo de' Fiori is the most Roman, most authentic of all the squares in the inner city. Right into the early modern period heretics were burned here – the speculative thinker Giordano Bruno, for instance, on February 17th 1600. A memorial to him stands in the square, and a commemorative ceremony is held there each year on the anniversary. Each morning there is a vegetable market, one of Rome's largest and best. About 2 pm the stalls are taken down and the superfluous greenery is gathered into great heaps – a rather strange sight. Excellent food in the little restaurants all round.

Campo de' Fiori – market

The Palazzo del Quirinale was begun in 1574 by Pope Gregory XIII to provide a cooler summer residence than the stuffy Vatican palace, and later became the popes' permanent residence. During Napoleon's campaign the palace was refurbished for the Emperor, but he never reached Rome again and in 1815 the popes moved back in – until 1870, when the king of Italy, Victor Emmanuel II, took up residence (the Pope fled to the Vatican as a 'voluntary prisoner'). Since 1946, when Italy became a republic, the palace and annexes have served as the residence of the president of Italy, though not all have actually wanted to live there. On June 2nd each year, Republic Day, there is a great official reception in the splendid formal gardens; nowadays it is by no means impossible for a foreigner to obtain an invitation.

Suggested tours of the city

Walking through Ancient Rome

A view from the summit of the Capitol over the superb ruins of the Roman forum: that's really how the exploration of the city of Rome should begin. But since you can't be magically whisked up there, begin the day as early as possible at the foot of the steps (called *Cordonata*), designed by Guglielmo della Porta in 1537, that lead gently from the *Piazza Venezia* up to the Capitol. For Pope Paul III, Michelangelo drew up a design for the square (1536) with three Renaissance palaces, the *Palazzo dei Conservatori* (on the right), *Palazzo Senatorio* (ahead) and *Palazzo Nuovo*. He also arranged for the ancient equestrian statue of the Emperor Marcus Aurelius (AD 160–87), raising his hand over Rome in salutation, to be removed from St John Lateran and set up here (1538). It was to be the focus of the entire square. (The statue, like many others, has recently been restored. It now stands in a glass case in the courtyard of the Palazzo Nuovo. Since 1982 the government has invested considerable sums to save Rome's archaeological treasures, many of which were until recently wrapped in green plastic tarpaulin. The chief cause of decay is atmospheric pollution arising from motor traffic.)

The Fora

On first sighting the Forum Romanum, you may have a moment's sympathy with the view of the young American William Dean Howells, who, on his visit in 1864, saw only 'incoherent columns overthrown and mixed with dilapidated walls'. But before descending the narrow stairway to the left of the Palazzo Senatorio to walk to the entrance of the *Forum Romanum* and the *Palatine*, one should try to make the same effort of imagination as Shelley, who, on his extended visit to Rome in the spring of 1819, came practically every day to walk in these ruins. 'Come to Rome: it is a scene by which expression is overpowered; which words cannot convey,' he wrote to Thomas Love Peacock. Recall that here was the heart of Republican and later Imperial Rome. Once a marsh between the four hills on which the primitive settlements stood, the Forum Romanum was drained in the 6th c. BC and in the course of time adorned with important buildings: the *Basilica Fulvia* of 179 BC (wrongly called the Basilica Aemilia), the sole surviving Republican basilica, and the *Basilica Iulii* (Julius Caesar), temples of *Saturn*, of *Concord*, and of *Castor and Pollux*, the Arches of Augustus and Septimius Severus, the temples of Julius Caesar, Vespasian and Antoninus Pius and his wife Faustina, the round temple of Vesta and the house of the Vestal Virgins...

The political centre of Republican Rome was also here: the Senate met in the *Curia* (rebuilt by Mussolini); the XII Tables, the first law-code of Rome (traditional date 451–450 BC), were inscribed on bronze tablets on the Republican *Rostra* (speaking-platform). The open spaces between the buildings served as an assembly for the citizens, as a market, as a court of justice. The main street of the Forum, the *Via Sacra*, led up to the Capitol. As Rome grew in importance, further fora and markets were built extending west and north-west, towards the slope of the Quirinal Hill (by Julius Caesar, Augustus, Vespasian, Nerva and, most magnificently, Trajan).

The Forum Romanum

For a thousand years the Roman Forum – enclosed by the Imperial palace on the Palatine, the Capitol, the Market of Trajan, the massive walls of the Forum of Augustus, and to the south-east the mighty curve of the Colosseum – was the showplace and epitome of Roman life and world supremacy. A vast basilica, whose central nave was 80 m long and 30 m wide, was built there by Maxentius and Constantine. The last official act took place in AD 608. Then the pomp slid into the gloom of the Dark Ages, as Rome became depopulated after the barbarian invasions and the destruction of the water supply (all the aqueducts were out of commission between 549 and 776). Warring city clans built their strongholds in the ruins of the ancient buildings; others were turned into churches. When the city's fortunes revived in the Renaissance, the fallen marbles of the Forum were used for building-stone and also burned as a source of lime for mortar, especially once Pope Paul III in 1540 gave the *Fabrica* of St Peter's the monopoly of all profits on the 'excavation' of ancient monuments. Eventually, as a thick covering of grass grew over the unremembered history of the Roman Empire, the place became a cattle pasture. The Forum Romanum was called *Campo Vaccino* (Ox Plain). Only in the 19th c. did archaeologists, above all

Interior of the Colosseum

Giacomo Boni and Rodolfo Lanciani, rediscover the great monuments of the past. (Lanciani wrote a number of still interesting books in English, e.g. *Ancient Rome in the Light of Modern Discoveries*, *The Ruins and Excavations of Ancient Rome*, and *Wanderings in the Roman Campagna*.)

Palatine, Colosseum and Forum Boarium

From the *Forum Romanum* you can mount directly up to the imperial palaces (of Augustus, Tiberius and Domitian) on top of the Palatine hill (the word 'palace' is of course derived ultimately from *palatium*, the imperial residence on the Palatine). The Palatine houses of the Republican aristocrats, including Cicero, were mainly situated on the slope of this hill immediately above the Temple of Vesta. In the Renaissance, the whole area was occupied by the Villa Farnesina and its gardens, by Vignola. From the far side, one can look down on the *Circus Maximus* (begun in 329 BC; the visible track dates from Trajan's reconstruction, when it could hold 250,000 spectators), in the trough separating the Palatine from the Aventine opposite. Off to the right in a small hollow, the ancient *Velabrum*, is the *Forum Boarium*, where cattle were shipped off the Tiber into the Roman market.

Descending the Palatine back into the Forum, you continue down the basalt paving slabs of the *Via Sacra* to the Arch of Titus, one of whose passage panels shows the triumph celebrating the Sack of Jerusalem in AD 70. From there, it is just a step out of the Forum to the Arch of Constantine and the Colosseum (dedicated AD 80).

To reach the *Forum Boarium*, it is simplest to return along the *Via Sacra*, out of the Forum Romanum and down the *Via di S. Teodoro*. In the centre is the double Arch of Constantine, and nearby the small Arch of the Argentarii (AD 204), newly restored. This stands in the shadow of *S. Giorgio in Velabro*, a fine early (7th c.) basilican church. Nearby are *S. Maria in Cosmedin* and the two best-preserved Antique temples in Rome, that of *Portunus* (formerly but inaccurately known as the temple of *Fortuna Virilis*) and the round temple probably dedicated to *Hercules Olivarius (Victor)*, which is the oldest marble building that survives in Rome. Further north (up the Tiber) are the grand ruins of the *Theatre of Marcellus* (dedicated by Augustus in 13 or 11 BC).

Baths of Caracalla

You may still have the stamina and interest to push on down the *Circus Maximus*, below the retaining walls of the Palatine, to the massive ruins of the Baths of Caracalla (the Antonine Baths, c. AD 212–216; bus no. 90 from the Colosseum or about twenty minutes on foot). Of these baths Shelley wrote: 'Never was any desolation so sublime and lovely.' The Opera holds its open-air performances of popular operas (above all *Aida*) here. Even if the acoustics are not ideal and the singers leave a bit to be desired, the play of lights on the vast craggy walls amid rustling pines and oleanders beneath the star-strewn sky is truly impressive. (Take a warm blanket with you: it gets cold by midnight!)

Via Appia Antica

From the Antonine Baths it takes about a quarter of an hour to reach the Aurelian Wall at *Porta San Sebastiano*. Here is the beginning of the *Via Appia Antica*, the 'Queen of Roads'. Today she is finding it hard to fight off the traffic and the speculative builders. The best advice is to put the first stretch behind one by taking bus no. 218 as far as it goes, and, first time round, to view the *Tomb of Caecilia Metella*, the *Domine Quo Vadis* chapel and the entrance to the *Catacombs of St Callistus* through the bus window. From the last halt a truly lovely walk lies before you (and before that, the possibility of eating lunch in one of the little restaurants in the neighbourhood of the stop). How far into the Campagna countryside along the Via Appia Antica your feet want to take you is an entirely individual decision. Not until you get to *Ciampino* airport, halfway to the Alban Hills (about 12 km), does the ancient road lose itself in scrub and undergrowth.

Such strength as remains for the return journey should be expended enjoyably on the places bypassed earlier (Catacombs, etc.). Of course the whole trip can be taken in two instalments: you eat lunch and take a siesta in the city, then explore the Via Appia Antica; then, perhaps after an excellent supper (*Escargot* or *S. Callisto* near the Tomb of Caecilia Metella), draw your long 'ancient day' to a close by attending the opera in the Antonine Baths.

Combining art and shopping

You can only grasp how grandly and elegantly the *Spanish Steps* sweep up to *S. Trinità dei Monti* bright and early, when no one is about. You may have to pick your way over a few sleeping backpackers, who populate the steps all day long. Apart from that, all is still soundless and deserted as you look from the *Obelisk* in front of the church down along the shadowed gorge of the *Via Condotti*, the most elegant of the numerous shopping streets that our tour includes.

Villa Borghese

The road up the side of the Pincio (*Viale della Trinità dei Monti*) beckons first, past the *Villa Medici* (the French Academy of Art) and the shallow fountain with the view out over to the dome of St Peter's, which once inspired so many Romantic painters, to the Pincio itself.

The Italian architect Giuseppe Valadier (1762–1839) created the splendid ramp with fountains between the *Piazza del Popolo* and the *Pincio terrace*, which is a sort of preliminary to the park of the *Villa Borghese*, in the former gardens of the Augustinian friars. The great Borghese park, with its pines and evergreen oaks, its artificial lakes, its little fortlets and its riding paths, is quite empty in the morning, and gives a slight hint of the peaceful, garden-filled Rome that the German historian Gregorovius, who lived in the city last century, mourned so bitterly. It was here that Keats took his last walks before his death in 1821.

Villa Borghese lake

Twin churches in the Piazza del Popolo

Piazza del Popolo

When you get down to the Piazza del Popolo (also designed by Valadier, from 1784) after your excursion in the Borghese gardens, it is worth looking into the church of *S. Maria del Popolo* (built by Pope Sixtus IV, 1462–65), just inside the *Porta del Popolo*, whose decoration was improved by Bernini in 1656 for the entry of Queen Christina of Sweden.

In the Cerasi chapel to the left of the high altar you can admire two of the finest Caravaggios (*The Conversion of St Paul, The Crucifixion of St Peter*, 1600–01); note too the Pinturicchio chapel beside the entrance, the chapel of Agostino Chigi designed by Raphael c. 1515, and Bramante's windows in the choir.

In the meantime the shopkeepers in the three main streets that radiate from the obelisk in the centre of the square (*Via del Babuino, Via del Corso, Via di Ripetta*) will have brushed the dust from their doorways and be awaiting custom.

Where to shop

If you are after antiques or modern art, then you must do the rounds in the *Via del Babuino*, and in the artists' street, *Via Margutta*, that lies parallel but hidden away behind. For smart clothes off the peg, handbags and shoes, there's really too much choice in the *Via del Corso*. Towards the end of the *Via della Ripetta* with its unassuming little shops, a square beckons: the monumental remains of the *Mausoleum of Augustus* (before 23 BC), topped with flowering oleanders. Over the road, protected by Mussolini from wind and weather in 1938, lies the *Ara Pacis*, the Altar of Peace, a triumph of Roman sculpture in Carrara marble. Dedicated by Augustus on June 9th 9 BC, it is a majestic religious and political monument to the Roman conception of the State.

Going south from here down the *Via della Scrofa*, across the northern part of the ancient *Campus Martius*, you pass the smaller Tiber-facing frontage of the great *Palazzo Borghese* and, from the main entrance in *Piazza della Fontanella Borghese*, admire the splendid garden court inside. The palace was acquired by Camillo Borghese, Pope Paul V, who gave it in 1613 to his nephew, Marcantonio Borghese (1598–1658). Like much of the property of the Borghese, including the contents of the Villa, it had to be disposed of in the 1890s.

Now cross over the Via del Corso into the *Via Condotti*, where you can wander at will in the pedestrian zone (which extends from the *Via della Croce* to *Via Frattina*) amid the rows of boutiques. The posters announcing 'Saldi' and 'Occasioni' make known that the summer sales have begun before summer

The elephant obelisk

itself has properly begun, and the winter sales can scarcely wait for Christmas.

If you are only going in for window-shopping, you will reach the *Piazza Colonna* unencumbered with parcels. In it are the *Column of Marcus Aurelius* (AD 180–96), with its spiral bas-reliefs illustrating the Emperor's wars against the Germans, and a Baroque fountain. This is the political centre of Italy: the terracotta-coloured *Palazzo Chigi* houses the prime minister's office, and a few steps away is the parliament building, the *Palazzo di Montecitorio*, designed originally by Bernini for the Ludovisi family (1650) and later completed as a papal court of justice (1697). Round about are the head offices of all the important Italian newspapers.

In the *Caffè Giolitti* (*Via Uffici del Vicario*) you will certainly bump into one or two members of parliament, busy, like you, fortifying themselves towards further efforts with one or two of Rome's finest ices.

The Pantheon

You come now to the *Pantheon*, the sole free-standing Antique building in Rome (AD 118–25) to survive complete, walls, roof and all (it was turned into a church, *S. Maria ad Martyres*, in AD 609). Raphael is buried here. The building is currently being restored.

Behind the Pantheon is *S. Maria sopra Minerva*, where Fra Angelico is buried. In the *piazza* in front of the church are the little elephant (carrying an obelisk) designed by a pupil of Bernini (1667) and the *Hotel Minerva*, where Stendhal lived in the 1830s.

Piazza Navona

It is now urgent to find an agreeable spot for a quiet lunch: the *Piazza Navona*. Hurrying on your way there, you will have glanced admiringly at the long façade, along the *Corso del Rina-scimento*, of the *Palazzo Madama* (once the seat of the Medici, but named after 'Madam' Margaret of Austria, the natural daughter of Charles V), now the Italian Senate (upper house of parliament). Once you have got a table at one of the four (not particularly cheap) restaurants, you can observe that the Piazza Navona is a complete Roman Baroque synthesis of the arts, built into the extended oval of Domitian's original stadium (completed in AD 86) in the *Campus Martius* by Girolamo Rainaldi (1570–1655). Since cars were banned, the piazza has been restored to Romans and foreigners, children and the 'artists' who hawk their work there. No traffic noise, just happy voices, the twittering of swallows, the plashing of water! No wonder that there are people in the Piazza Navona day and night all year round.

The little streets in the area are still inhabited by ordinary Romans, even though the craftsmen's workshops are slowly but surely giving way to commerce. The nearby *Via dei Coronari* was the first to make the change, and has turned itself into a permanent antiques market (pedestrian zone). Right and left all the way along the street numerous little alleys give on to smart courtyards or tumbledown areas, until you finally reach the Tiber and the Ponte S. Angelo.

Round about the Campo de' Fiori

If you go back along the *Corso Vittorio Emanuele*, there is still a fine choice of buildings to stop and look at, above all the imposing *Palazzo della Cancelleria*, the papal court of justice and administrative building, which is a rather severe example of early Renaissance architecture (1484–1511). Its building by the

Fountains in the Piazza Navona

nephew of Pope Sixtus IV marked the beginning of Rome's revival. Crossing the *Campo de' Fiori* (where the most colourful of Rome's vegetable markets is held each weekday morning) you come to the *Piazza Farnese*, in front of the *Palazzo Farnese* (mostly 1515–49), which was built by da Sangallo the Younger, Michelangelo and others for Cardinal Alessandro Farnese, later Pope Paul III (1534–49). It may be said to be the high point of palace building in Rome, everywhere suggestive of size, space and grandeur. (It now houses the French Embassy and Archaeological School in Rome.)

Caffè Greco

The *Via Giulia* (laid out by Pope Julius II before 1512), once the foremost street of Rome and now still a smart place to live, passes behind the Palazzo Farnese. It will take you back to the social and business centre of Rome. Having enjoyed so much art, you deserve something for the flesh: have a drink in the *Caffè Greco*, named after a former Greek coffee-maker in the Via Condotti whose premises were frequented by Goethe, Byron, Beethoven, Wagner and so on; then go to a *trattoria* (such as *Otello*, Via della Croce) or a smart restaurant (such as *Ranieri*, Via Mario di Fiori). And then you'll be back where you started, at the *Piazza di Spagna*.

A visit to the Vatican

If one wished to delve thoroughly into the Vatican City and its secrets, one truly would out-pope the Pope, who is far too occupied with his high office to be able to stroll in his gardens or walk through his museums and palaces.

The best time to arrive at St Peter's or the Vatican Museums is around 8 am;

already by 9 am the square becomes busy and there are long queues forming.

St Peter's Square

When you walk into St Peter's Square you are already just outside the territory of the tiny state of the Vatican City, which has only 44,000 sq m and around 1,000 inhabitants. It is superfluous to urge you to surrender yourself first of all to the impact (or rather the embrace) of this space confined by Bernini's dense *colonnades* (1656–67). The 140 saints' statues gaze out at you, the water plashes in the fountains on either side of the obelisk (the largest in Rome after that of the Lateran), and even the group of pilgrims' coaches looks tiny on this scale. The broad stone ramp gently leads one up to the portico of *St Peter's*.

St Peter's

The art historians have spilled a great deal of ink over the question whether Carlo Maderna's additional two bays and façade (1606–14) ruined Michelangelo's design of a Greek cross with dome. At any rate, from dawn to dusk the wide-open bronze portal by the Florentine Filarete bids us enter inside. In the 'Holy Year' (AD 2000) the fifth door, the *Porta Santa* on the right-hand side, is to be open, and then closed again for twenty-five years.

One cannot actually inspect St Peter's: one can merely pay it a visit, during which one wanders about in its vast interior, with devout or secular astonishment according to one's nature. Over the centuries, the feet of the bronze statue of the chief Apostle, Peter (on the right, just before the transept), have become quite worn and polished by the hands (and lips) of the pious.

Right: St Peter's

Beneath the dome, as the archaeologists proved conclusively some years ago, lies the Apostle's tomb. 'Thou art Peter, and upon this rock I will build my Church...and I will give unto thee the keys of the kingdom of heaven' (*Matth.* 16.18–19) stands written in Latin in large mosaic letters round the base of the dome.

Should one give all the dimensions of the cathedral? Or does it suffice to say that Bernini's golden baldachin over the high altar is as tall as the Palazzo Farnese (29 m – 95 ft!)? And that the church covers one and a half hectares of land (3.7 acres)? Even the plump marble putti that adorn one of the numerous well-known tombs are larger than we. Before hastening by the lift or on foot up the wide spiral staircase to the roof of the church (the ticket office is outside, to the right of the building), have a look at the three sacristies (the general sacristy, the sacristy of the canons with the chapter-house, and the prebendaries' sacristy) on the way to *St*

Inside the Vatican

Peter's Treasury. The best pieces were plundered in 1527 by the German troops of the Duke of Bourbon in the Sack of Rome, and in 1797 Napoleon carried off other valuables; there still is, though, among other pieces, a dalmatic that Charlemagne is supposed to have worn in 800 when he was crowned in Old St Peter's.

On the roof, the cupola is near enough to touch. You can even go up it, for in the space between the two skins of the dome stairs lead up to the lantern, Rome's peerless belvedere. Down below are St Peter's Square, the Vatican palaces and the gardens. All Rome lies at your feet.

It was on the roof of St Peter's that a famous incident took place (1817) concerning Lord Byron, after he had left England in disgrace: Lady Liddell, with her four daughters, caught sight of him, and cried out, 'Don't look at him, he is dangerous to look at!'

The Vatican Grottos

You should now, and not merely for the sake of the contrast, descend beneath St Peter's to the *Vatican Grottos*. The entrance is near the baldachin, in one of the piers supporting the dome. The extensive cemetery lies on two, or rather three, levels: the New Grottos, the Old Grottos and the ancient necropolis with the tomb of St Peter. This last was originally just a trench, and was turned into a simple monumental tomb in the middle of the 2nd c. AD. The name Peter is written in Greek on the back wall of the tomb. Cool, eerie and awe-inspiring.

An audience with the Pope

The next step in your papal excursion depends on which day of the week it is, and what time. Each Wednesday the Pope's official audience takes place in

The Vatican gardens

the big modern audience-chamber behind the building of the Holy Office. To be allowed in, you must on the Tuesday morning get yourself admitted by the Swiss Guards at the bronze door to the office of the *Maestro di Camera*, where you obtain an entrance ticket (9 am – 1 pm, first floor, entrance beneath the colonnade). The public audience often takes place in summer in St Peter's Square; then you do not need an entrance ticket.

The Vatican gardens

Viewing the Vatican gardens, which used only to be possible by obtaining special permission, grudgingly given, is nowadays a new source of income for the Vatican. You go to the information office, on the left of the square, and join a group (tel. 6982). Tours of the Vatican City and gardens are conducted during the morning for groups of around forty people. The tours last about three hours. Remember to catch from the gardens the view of the cupola of St Peter's, which gives you the effect intended by Bramante and Michel-angelo.

If you would like to provide yourself with Vatican stamps, you may do so in the Vatican post office to the right of the bronze door of St Peter's. In summer, two portable post offices stand on the right of the square. Given the proverbial inefficiency of the Italian postal system, everyone posts their foreign mail, especially urgent mail, in the Vatican. You would do well to do the same with your postcards.

The Vatican Museums

The only part of the papal palace that the tourist is permitted to see is the part which houses the rambling *Vatican Museums*. The collections and the decorated saloons are extremely impressive and generally swarming with tourists. For that reason, in summer strict control is maintained with the help of entrance barriers. You are thus channelled through the *Sistine Chapel*, the *Borgia apartments*, the *Stanze of Raphael*, and also the *Egyptian, Etruscan, Graeco-Roman* and (since recently) *modern collections*; there is little time for contemplative reverie. If you are a connoisseur of art, you have more freedom of movement in the winter months. (Even then, however, you are advised to arrive early.) The entrance fee is quite stiff.

Around the Vatican

It would be better use of a nice sunny day to view the *Castel Sant'Angelo* – and certainly *not* by following the monumental *Via della Conciliazione*, which Mussolini laid out to seal the Lateran Pact of 1929, demolishing in order to do so a picturesque neighbourhood of little alleyways in front of the square.

Borgo Pio

Follow the old wall in the direction of the *Castel Sant'Angelo* from the northern colonnade of St Peter's Square, glancing into the old *Borgo*, where in the Middle Ages pilgrims and mercenaries stayed. During the frequent wars and sieges, cardinals and popes fled through the little passageway in this wall to the protection of the Castel, then moated by the Tiber.

Horse-drawn cabs in St Peter's Square

Castel Sant'Angelo

Visiting the Castel Sant'Angelo (once Hadrian's mausoleum) is a journey through two millennia. It offers incomparable views. From here, it takes just a few minutes to walk along the Tiber to the *Via del Gianicolo*, past the old *S. Spirito* hospital (originally an English foundation). This broad road rises up to the highest vantage-point over the inner city, the *Piazza Garibaldi* (twenty minutes on foot, or bus no. 41, every quarter of an hour from *Largo Tassoni* on the *Corso Vittorio Emanuele*). It's better to walk, because on foot you can take picturesque short-cuts (*Salita di S. Onofrio*) and use *S. Onofrio*, the monastery of St Jerome, as a half-way stopping place. The author of *Gerusalemme Liberata*, the poet Torquato Tasso, died here (1595). The rotten stump of the famous oak under which he sat and wrote is 200 m further on, and not far away is a flourishing offspring.

The Tiber and the Ponte Vittorio Emanuele from the Castel Sant'Angelo

Gianicolo (Janiculum)

The hill shelters a little open-air theatre, the *Gianicolo*, where performances of Latin classics (Plautus, for example) are put on in summer. Above it, the *Faro*, a marble lighthouse, flashes the Italian colours, green, white and red, over the capital by night; it was a gift of the poor emigrants from the south who wished to mark their homesickness for Italy. Then you reach the summit and with it the showy *Garibaldi Monument*. Summer and winter, day and night, the *Piazzale Giuseppe Garibaldi* is where the Romans meet, the tourist buses stop, the souvenir- and balloon-hawkers ply their trade. The broad roadway continues down to the *Fontanone*, the gigantic terminal fountain of the *Acqua Paola*, which Pope Paul V had rebuilt out of Trajan's ancient aqueduct, the *Aqua Traiana*. The water comes 43 km right

across the northern Campagna from Lake Bracciano.

Descent to Trastevere

Carrying on down the *Via Garibaldi* you reach the *Piazza S. Pietro in Montorio*, a broad esplanade in front of the Spanish Academy and the façade of the Renaissance church *S. Pietro in Montorio*. Of an evening, the inhabitants of crowded Trastevere take a breath of air here, and play *boccia* (bowls) while the children romp about. As a popular place to get married, the church is constantly overloaded with flowers. It contains in the first chapel on the left a fine fresco (*Flagellation of Christ*) by Sebastiano del Piombo. But it is famous for containing, in the cloister, Bramante's miniature masterpiece the *Tempietto* (after 1502), erected on the spot where St Peter was supposed to have been crucified. If you go round to the back of the Tempietto, you can gain access to an underground shrine, in which the site of the martyr-dom is visible beneath a glass plate let into the floor.

To conclude the day, take the steps from the Piazza down to Trastevere – which has a section to itself.

A summer evening in Trastevere

There is no need to feel sorry for anyone who takes a holiday in Rome during the *canicola*, the Dog-days. Up-to-date Romans and lovers of Rome are begin-ning to swim against the current, and not quit the town all of a sudden like everyone else, but are learning instead to relish their rediscovery of the city even at this hot, deserted time. The hottest period of the *canicola* coincides with two festivals: the *Festa di Noantri*, the popular festival of Trastevere, whose inhabitants have always felt themselves more Roman than the Romans; and the *Ferragosto*, the *Feriae Augustae*, since the days of the Emper-or Augustus the ultimate three-day holi-day for loafing about.

The Festa di Noantri

This lasts an entire week, starting on the last Saturday in July. It begins with the ceremonial procession in honour of the Virgin, preceded by a brass band and including the city fathers, who get no less sweaty than the men carrying the statue: 6 o'clock in the evening (actually 5 o'clock, because of summer time) means, in Rome, that it's boiling hot. The people of Trastevere follow on behind praying and singing out of tune, and others lean out over the window-sills, which are decorated with rugs. In the evening, dotted all over the district, are programmes of band-stand music and every sort of competition (extempore poetry, for instance), but above all gar-

gantuan drinking and feasting in the open air.

The entire immense district is crammed with wooden tables and chairs, amid hundreds of fairground booths, merry-go-rounds, shooting-stalls, etc. – a Roman equivalent of Not-tingham Goosefair, but much simpler, noisier and in every respect more unre-strained. Not a soul remains indoors: toddlers and ancients join the party. *Porchetta*, whole roast pig stuffed with pungent herbs, Frascati wine and water-melon fuel the whole thing; you have to join in just to escape going under in the scramble.

Piazza S. Maria in Trastevere

Luckily for foreigners, there is an entire area of 'better' restaurants round the medieval *Piazza dei Mercanti* (near S. Cecilia). Here the frantic summer festiv-ities assume a more polished air. There are also plenty of gourmet restaurants around the *Piazza di S. Maria in Traste-vere*, with its gigantic Baroque fountain (remodelled by Bernini in 1659).

During the *Festa*, it will take at least half the night to explore all the thronged alleyways and squares. Only in the early morning does it get a bit quieter on the carnage-field of fleshly delights – and then in the dim light of dawn the dust-men, with heavy hearts, set about clear-ing up the mountains of rubbish and shooing off the cats and dogs gnawing the pig skulls and bones.

You can of course only view the fine churches from the outside during the nights of the festival. So in the afternoon you should at least inspect *S. Maria in Trastevere* (the light is best then), with its famous mosaics of the life of the Virgin by Cavallini and its splendid floors; and, at the other end of Trastevere, near the Porta Portese, Bernini's stunning final masterpiece (1674), a reclining marble figure of the beatified Ludovica Albertoni, in *S. Francesco a Ripa*. There is only one time in the week you can view the remnants of Cavallini's vast fresco of the *Last Judgement* with the iridescent angels' wings (c. 1293) in *S. Cecilia*, the third of Trastevere's important churches: ring on Sunday morning at 11 am at the entrance to the cloister, on the left of the entrance to the church (closed August).

The ghetto and the surrounding area

But now back to Trastevere by night. If you go back home on foot, go via the two old bridges that cross the Tiber island, with its little square fronted by *S. Bartolomeo* and medieval houses. Over the other side is the Synagogue, protecting the ghetto, which nowadays thank goodness is no longer a restricted quarter as it was in former times. Here too, the most agreeable time to wander is at night, when all is quiet – the old alleys, and the *Portico of Octavia* (what remains visible dates from the Severan rebuilding of AD 203), which is now the porch of *S. Angelo in Pescheria*. But especially worth noting are the elaborate turtle-fountain in the *Piazza Mattei* and the façades of the fine palaces that rise amid the jumble of ordinary houses. At the end of the *Via delle Botteghe Oscure* (the Street of the Dark Shops), where once the cloth-wholesalers, who were forbidden in the ghetto, carried on their trade in secret, and which is now a good place for shopping, you can see the illuminated *Capitol* up to the right, and to the north the *Palazzo Venezia*. And there you are, back in the heart of Classical Rome.

Discovering Byzantine and medieval Rome

You begin your exploration in front of the *Basilica S. Maria Maggiore*, which,

after lengthy restoration work over the past years, can now once again be admired from the inside. The finest part is the far end of the basilica, with its sweeping steps in front of the apse. Then you should walk the few steps across the piazza to the *Via S. Prassede*, which brings you to a side-entrance of *S. Prassede* church. There are many fine things to see, but the most important is the *Cappella di S. Zenone*, the Chapel of St Zeno. Pope Paschal I (817–42) had this tiny chapel, entirely covered in mosaics, built as a tomb for his mother Theodora. In marvellous shades of blue, red and green on a glittering gold background the majestic ancient faces gaze down on our prosaic existence; we stand spellbound in this pious shrine, brushed by a hint of the yearning Byzantine belief in Paradise.

S. Pudenziana

Close by this jewel, down from S. Maria Maggiore in the *Via Urbana*, stands *S. Pudenziana*, reputedly the oldest church in Rome, built over the house of the Roman senator Pudens. St Peter is supposed to have stayed there and converted the senator, together with his daughters Praxedis and Pudentiana, to the new faith. The mosaic in the apse, *Christ in majesty*, dates from the 5th c. and is one of the most important remains of Early Christian art. Part of the Roman house is preserved in the oratory.

At the end of the *Via Urbana*, you pass through the *Piazza degli Zingari* (Gypsy Square) to reach the *Largo Visconti Venosta*, not a place where you see many tourists. Here there are the remains of a fortified tower, and it is not far to Michelangelo's famous *Moses* in the church of *S. Pietro in Vincoli*.

As a pleasant variation, you may decide to take one of the numerous

S. Giovanni in Laterano – a 17th c. church with a 13th c. cloister

buses from the *Piazza S. Maria Maggiore* to the *Basilica S. Giovanni in Laterano* (St John Lateran), which retains its 13th c. cloister although the church itself was rebuilt in the 17th c. Next go down past the *Ospedale S. Giovanni* and into the *Via dei SS. Quattro Coronati.* The church of that name was founded in the 4th c. by four martyrs, either former Roman soldiers or, according to another account, quarrymen, from Pannonia. A large new building was erected on top in the 9th c.

S. Stefano Rotondo and the park of the Villa Celimontana

By taking a cross-street, the *Via Celimontana,* past the Ospedale del Celio you reach the *Via di S. Stefano Rotondo.* The famous 5th c. rotunda of S. Stefano (with later additions) has recently been reopened after twenty years of excavation and restoration (a *Temple of Mithras* was found beneath the floor). You are now very near the quiet *Via della Navicella,* named after the fountain in

the form of a boat in front of the doorway of *S. Maria in Domnica.* Cyriaca, a Roman matron, is supposed to have turned her house here into a Christian church in the 3rd c., on top of which Pope Paschal I had the basilica built. The (much restored) mosaics are probably to be seen as Paschal's response to the Iconoclastic movement in the Eastern Church. According to the inscription they 'shine like the light of Phoebus in the universe when he frees himself from the dark veils of obscure night'.

You are now in an area where gardens mingle harmoniously with shrines. The park of the *Villa Celimontana* is the least-known idyllic green island in Rome (with a splendid children's playground hidden away below). Turning left out of S. Maria in Domnica, you will see the monastery of *SS. Giovanni e Paolo* at the end of the narrow Via di S. Paolo della Croce. According to tradition, a senator named Byzantius and his son Pammachius, who had been converted to Christianity, built the original church around AD 400 on the site of a Roman house where, during the persecution under Julian the Apostate (360–63), two imperial officials, John and Paul, had been executed. Extensive parts of the earlier building have been uncovered, and in the *Clivus Scauri,* which runs outside, even the original cobblestones are visible. The Romanesque campanile stands on the walls of the vast *Temple of the divine Claudius,* which directly faced the Palatine. It was rebuilt by Vespasian (AD 69–80) after being partly demolished by Nero. Sometimes, in summer, ballet performances are given in the courtyard.

The three levels of S. Clemente

Take the *Viale del Parco Celio* past the Botanical Gardens almost to the Colosseum, but veering away from it into the

Via Capo d'Africa. Then left into the *Via Celimontana* again, and so to the church of *S. Clemente*, on the *Via S. Giovanni in Laterano*. This is the most important of the eighteen Titular Churches of Rome, the Christian places of worship which were recognised in 385 as having belonged to private individuals with good title ('titulus'). But visiting *S. Clemente* does not take you back merely to the beginnings of Christianity. In the Domitianic apartment block beneath the church there was a temple of Mithras (which can be visited) in a complex of rooms used as a bath-house.

This is the 'first level' of S. Clemente. The second is that of the 4th c. church. Its great treasures are the wall-paintings of the miracles of St Clement, and the 9th c. frescos of the Ascension, in the nave. Confident in their piety, the unknown artists claim in an inscription that these paintings are superior in point of beauty to all previous ones. The bright, powerful colours, forms and dress indicate a release from the stiffness of Byzantine art: these paintings are among the most important precursors of the Romanesque style.

The 4th c. church was destroyed in 1084. In the Upper Church, with its apse-mosaic (1118) and Cosmati-work, you come closer to our own period-sense. In the left aisle, the *Chapel of St Catherine* has very fine Renaissance frescos to offer, though it is debated whether they are by Masaccio (1401–?28) or his teacher, the Florentine Masolino (1383–1447).

You have now seen many of the little-known beauties of Byzantine and medieval Rome. Now for a quiet, well-furnished table: say, *Angelino's* on the corner of the *Via Cavour/Via dei Fori Imperiali*, or the roof-terrace of the nearby *Hotel Forum*.

Miscellaneous

Via del Corso

Rome's main street is almost 2 km long, linking the *Piazza del Popolo* to the *Piazza Venezia*. Since private cars have been banned from it and only public transport allowed, pedestrians have greater freedom. In former days, the Roman Carnival took place here, as well as the races between the (riderless) Berber stallions. The Corso was later where the purse-proud notables paraded daily in their carriages, watched by those who had to use Shanks's pony. On January 5th 1854 gas lighting was introduced, and the Pope, who then was also the secular lord of Rome, had the pedlars and kerb-cooks cleared from the street. Ever since, the Corso has been a smart place to shop. The department store *Magazzino Bocconi* was actually opened by King Umberto I. When it

The Via del Corso

changed hands after the First World War, they wanted to find a new name for the old store. The celebrated poet Gabriele d'Annunzio came up with one, *La Rinascente* – and received the then considerable prize of 5,000 lire.

No end of famous people have lived in the Via del Corso: Goethe, Canova, the Tzarina Catherine, Napoleon III, Federico Zuccari (1542/43–1609, the founder of the Accademia S. Luca), Pietro Mascagni (the composer of *Cavalleria Rusticana*, 1890) and many others. The Shelleys stayed in the Palazzo Verospi during their visit in 1819. Nowadays the street is lined with offices: banks, newspapers and insurance companies. Just off it, at the Piazza Venezia end (*1a Piazza del Collegio Romano*), is

The Caffè Greco

the entrance to the *Galleria Doria-Pamphili* (fine paintings). Higher up are a number of old churches, including *S. Lorenzo in Lucina* (with Bernini's *Cappella Fonseca* and Chateaubriand's monument to Poussin, who died in Rome in 1665), and several cinemas. Towards the Piazza del Popolo is the recently opened little *Goethe Museum* (no. 31). There are 531 house-numbers, not, as usual, ordered even on one side and odd the other, but continuously, down from the Piazza del Popolo and back again the other side.

Caffè Greco and Babington

In his memoirs, Antonio Canova devotes no fewer than fifty-seven pages to the celebrated *Antico Caffè Greco*, which is still today – unaltered – at 86 *Via Condotti*. Ten years ago it luckily escaped a crisis. The old proprietor went bankrupt and the café was supposed to be sold and modernised. But the government took a hand and prevented the old mirrors and stiff velvet armchairs and sofas from being removed. Today the Caffè Greco, fitted out just as in 1760, is a rendezvous for fashionable people to have a drink after going shopping.

Babington is the name of the high-class tea-shop immediately to the left of the Spanish Steps. A number of English travellers to Rome stayed in this area. John Keats spent his last months, and died, in the pink house (no. 26) just to the right of the steps (November 1820–February 1821), which is now the Keats-Shelley Memorial House. Lord Byron stayed at no. 66, practically opposite, during the spring of 1817, when he was gathering inspiration for the Fourth Canto of *Childe Harold*. J. M. W. Turner stayed at 12 Piazza Mignanelli during the winter of 1828–29, making numerous sketches and studies of Rome that are now in the Tate Gallery.

Even today one may still bump into English authors in *Babington*, all settled down to write. It is the only place in Rome where you can get a properly made cup of tea and hot buns or toast with butter and jam or marmalade – but it's very expensive!

Palazzo Farnese

Only if you have good contacts in the French Embassy (or have reason to use the library of the French School of Archaeology) can you get permission to inspect the *Palazzo Farnese* from inside. Failing that, there remains only the examination of the marvellous façade and the inner courtyard. The French state pays a symbolic annual rent of one lira. The contract expires in December 2035, having been signed in 1936 for ninety-nine years. The palace was built for Cardinal Alessandro Farnese. Queen Christina of Sweden moved in for a time in 1655 after her abdication, and later the Neapolitan Bourbons. The French Embassy was here already in 1870, and at the beginning of this century the French state acquired the palace. But the Italian state reserved for itself for twenty-five years the right to repurchase, and indeed made use of it. When it was bought back, however, the advantageous peppercorn rent was established for the sake of France's diplomatic representation.

The Cancelleria

Not far from the *Palazzo della Cancelleria*, off the *Corso Vittorio Emanuele*, in ancient times was the *Theatre of Pompey* (inaugurated in 55 BC), where Julius Caesar was assassinated in 44 BC. The *Palazzo*, begun in 1490 by Cardinal Raffaele Riario, the nephew of Sixtus IV, was the seat of the Apostolic Vice-Chancellor of the Catholic Church. Later, during the Napoleonic occupation, it was the criminal court of justice. Nowadays it houses the Apostolic Chancellery and the marriage annulment court, the *Sacra Romana Rota*.

S. Spirito Theatre

Off the *Borgo S. Spirito*, parallel to the Via della Conciliazione leading up to the Vatican, there is a special kind of theatre in the cellar of the church belonging to the S. Spirito hospital. Here, for several decades, the theatre company *Compagnia d'Origlia-Palmi* has performed its speciality, edifying and sentimental religious plays, mostly written by the company itself. You can watch the martyrdom of St Lawrence or the dramatic story of St Rita of Cascia (1381–1457, canonised 1900). The company is composed of the members of a large theatrical family. The actors appear generally in several roles. For a while, the theatre was patronised by Roman intellectuals, who vastly amused themselves at the primitive technique and naïveté of the plays. The present audience, though, consists of the inmates of church orphanages and convent schools, elderly people from Trastevere and so on. In summer, the cellar-theatre is a most welcomely cool place to visit, and it costs so ridiculously little to get in that you really should go. Quite apart from the pious melodrama, you will experience an aspect of Roman life in the ambience of the Church that is bound soon to disappear. You can find the programmes in the daily papers under the theatre announcements.

Rome: a classified directory

Museums and galleries

In recent times the famous Roman museums have unfortunately suffered a good deal. Municipality and government were acutely short of money, and this led to staff shortages that closed many museums entirely or in part. The situation has now improved greatly. Money has been found for renovation and for staffing, and the problems which until quite recently used to beset the visitor – notably museums being closed when theoretically they should have been open – have eased considerably. Nevertheless, to be on the safe side, before planning to visit a museum you would do best to enquire of the hotel porter, or by telephoning, whether, and when, that particular museum is open.

Fortunately, the whole of Rome is a museum that cannot be kept closed. The churches, the fountains, the Aurelian walls, the baths, the old alleys and Baroque palaces, courtyards and façades are all there for the asking, and anyone can visit them at any time. Besides, life pullulates through them and all about them, which makes them a bit less sterile and museum-like.

Here is a list of the most important Roman museums. The entrance prices depend on whether they belong to the state or to the municipality of Rome. All state museums are open on Sundays and are then also free. On Mondays, all museums in Rome and the surrounding area are closed.

The Capitoline Museum, divided between the *Palazzo dei Conservatori* (which also has a picture gallery on the second floor) and the *Palazzo Nuovo*: see page 26.

Museum of Etruscan Art, Villa Giulia, 9 Piazza di Villa Giulia (just down the Viale delle Belle Arti from the *Museum of Modern Art*, on the far side of the Villa Borghese): see page 26.

Etruscan sculpture in the Villa Giulia

The Baths of Diocletian Museum (*Museo Nazionale Romano alle Terme di Diocleziano*), in the Piazza dei Cinquecento (near the Termini Station), was originally formed to house ancient finds from excavations on public property within the city of Rome, but was enlarged in 1900 by the addition of the former Ludovisi collection (Museo Boncompagni). The sheer bulk of modern archaeological finds, however, combined with chronic shortage of cash and old-fashioned layout, makes a visit a trifle disappointing, even if the galleries are now more often open than shut.

Galleria Borghese, in the villa of the same name in the Borghese Gardens. On the ground floor there is a large collection of sculpture, including *Venus reclining*, the famous classicising statue by Canova, for which the model was Napoleon's sister Pauline, wife of Prince Camillo Borghese; and Bernini's *Apollo and Daphne* (1625). On the floor above is the picture gallery, with many Renaissance masterpieces, but unfortunately these cannot be seen at the moment as the museum is being restored. Only the ground floor is on view, though one or two pictures have been brought downstairs. Currently no charge!

Galleria Barberini, in the Palazzo Barberini, Via Quattro Fontane. This is one of the 'old-fashioned' museums in Rome, with the advantage that the life-style of the original princely inhabitants and art-collectors is faithfully preserved (though some modernisation has taken place recently). The collection contains pictures by Fra Angelico, Raphael, Piero della Francesca, Holbein and Caravaggio.

Museo Barracco, a museum of ancient sculpture, 168 Corso Vittorio Emanuele. A small but splendid private collection donated to the City of Rome, but unfortunately 'in restauro' at the moment and thus closed.

Palazzo Braschi, near neighbour of the Museo Barracco (just over the road), is the museum of the City of Rome, with a great deal of material on life in Rome in the Middle Ages and Early Modern period. The galleries have been well restored and are often the venue for large international exhibitions.

Four noble palaces house picture galleries that were in purely private possession but are now open to the public. All of them exhibit the paintings in the traditional (cramped!) manner:

Palazzo Colonna, 1 Via della Pilotta, is open only on Saturday mornings; pictures by Veronese, Tintoretto and Carlo Maratti.

Palazzo Doria-Pamphili, 1a Piazza del Collegio Romano, still privately owned by the family, so that the modernisation of the galleries is the more praiseworthy. Nowadays, one can also visit the private apartments. Don't miss Velázquez's portrait of Pope Innocent X or Caravaggio's *Rest on the Flight into Egypt*.

Palazzo Spada, 3 Piazza Capodiferro (near the Palazzo Farnese). Its main interest, besides a small collection of paintings, is the Mannerist architecture. You can view the inner court; beyond it is a second court with *colonnades* by Borromini, whose foreshortened perspective offers a masterpiece of illusionistic Baroque architecture.

Palazzo Corsini, Via della Lungara (near the Villa Farnesina below the Gianicolo), which was once the residence of Queen Christina of Sweden, is now the *Accademia dei Lincei*, the Italian equivalent of the British Academy. In the upper saloons is a small but attractive collection (Caravaggio), owned by the State.

Castel Sant'Angelo is, quite apart from its historical and architectural interest, also a museum, containing above all frescos, and a great collection of old weaponry. The Emperor Hadrian built the vast pile as a mausoleum, the popes turned it into a fortress, using it occasionally as a dungeon. Benvenuto Cellini, the famous goldsmith, describes in his imaginative autobiography how he escaped from the castle. On Sundays, Roman families, down to the dog, love exploring the winding terraces of this multi-storeyed monument. (See also page 17.)

Calcografia: the name of the Museum of Prints and Drawings, 44 Via del Sudario. The building is by Giuseppe Valadier.

Palazzo Venezia, 3 Piazza Venezia: the most noteworthy sections are a

The Cortile della Pigna at the Vatican Museum

small but interesting exhibit of 14th and 15th c. pictures (Giovanni Bellini, Simone Martini, Dürer, etc.) and an extensive decorative and applied art collection (ivories, weapons, tapestries). In another part of this vast edifice (where Mussolini installed his office) large international exhibitions are held.

Vatican Museums: see page 26.

Museo della Civiltà Romana, in the Universal Exhibition area, EUR: see page 27.

Museum of Modern Art, whose official name is *Galleria Nazionale d'Arte Moderna*, 131 Via delle Belle Arti (up the road from the Villa Giulia). In the past few years this museum has changed completely: the vast florid canvases of the 19th and early 20th c. have been exiled to a side wing. The main galleries house the recent acquisitions of abstract art, from the Cubists to the avantgardists whose work one otherwise sees at the *Biennale* in Venice or the *Documenta* in Kassel. But the collection is mainly instructive about modern art in Italy. There generally has not been enough money to buy French, German or American art. However, the entire intelligentsia of Rome turns out to the openings of international peripatetic exhibitions of modern art.

If you get as far as the Museum of Modern Art, you should certainly take a couple of minutes to view the next building down, in the *Piazza Winston Churchill* (the tip of *Via Antonio Gramsci*), Edwin Lutyens's splendid classical edifice, which houses the *British School at Rome* (archaeology and fine arts). Thomas Ashby, one of the early directors (1906–25), was a passionate photographer, and made a unique archive of photographs of the old Campagna before it was irremediably ruined.

✝ Churches of Rome

There is probably no need to explain why, as a visitor to Rome, you should be constantly sent off to visit churches, even if you are not particularly devout. The history, and art history, of Rome is inscribed in her more than 350 churches. Of course, only the most important can be mentioned here. Please observe the request affixed to every church door, that you enter the house of God in respectable clothes, neither scanty nor diaphanous. It is not appropriate to call attention to oneself by sightseeing when a service is in progress.

S. Agnese in Agone, on the Piazza Navona, built by Francesco Borromini (1653–57). It dominates the long side of the square, and, according to legend, occupies the spot where St Agnes before her martyrdom was to have been brought naked to face the crowd, but miraculously was covered by her long hair. She was then beheaded. In front of the façade, Borromini's rival Bernini erected the *Fountain of the Four Rivers* (1651), all four of which turn their backs on it, evidently to express their dismay at the 'frightful' façade. For his part, Borromini set up his statue of St Agnes in the middle of the façade, to outface the insult.

S. Agnese fuori le Mura, 324 Via Nomentana: see page 71.

S. Agostino, Piazza S. Agostino, with a Renaissance façade, late 15th c. This church contains a statue by Sansovino, the *Madonna del Parto* (1521), famous among the women of Rome as the protector of those who are pregnant. In the nave is a fresco by Raphael, the *Prophet Isaiah* (1512); high altar by Bernini. In the first side-chapel on the left is a famous painting by Caravaggio, *La Madonna dei Pellegrini* (1612).

S. Andrea al Quirinale, over the road from the Quirinal Palace, was built by Bernini in 1678. He considered that the elliptical, salon-like little church was one of his happiest architectural inspirations.

S. Andrea della Valle in the Corso Vittorio Emanuele, the church of the Clerks Regular (Theatines), contains the splendid tombs of Popes Pius II (removed from St Peter's) and III (who died ten days after his coronation). The enormous cupola, the largest in Rome after St Peter's, is visible from afar over the roofs. A number of architects built the church between 1591 and 1665 (Early Baroque). The *Cappella Attavani*, first on the right, designed by Carlo Fontana, is the scene of the first act of Puccini's *Tosca*.

S. Cecilia in Trastevere is one of the Early Christian churches built on the foundations of a Roman house (that of St Cecilia). Later rebuilt several times. Note a Gothic tabernacle on the high altar. Most worth a visit however is Pietro Cavallini's fresco *The Last Judgement*, which was partly destroyed by later building work. It is in the gallery, which is part of the Benedictine convent, and can only be seen on Sunday mornings at 11 am.

S. Cesareo, Via di Porta S. Sebastiano, built before 1192, contains perhaps the finest Cosmati-work in Rome: pulpit, *schola cantorum* and baldachin. Its careful restoration in the late 15th c. is interesting historically, as one of the first signs of an awakening concern with Roman Christianity of the earlier period.

S. Clemente, Via S. Giovanni in Laterano (see pages 18, 58). S. Clemente is one of the four Irish churches in Rome.

SS. Cosma e Damiano, near the entrance to the Forum Romanum. What was probably the library of the Severan rebuilding of the *Templum Pacis* was turned into a Christian church in the 6th c. and rebuilt in the 17th c. Splendid mosaics in the apse, from the earlier period.

S. Crisogono, Piazza Sidney Sonnino, Trastevere, a repeatedly rebuilt Early Christian church. The campanile dates from the 12th c. Especially arresting inside are twenty-two ancient Ionic

S. Giovanni in Laterano

columns made of granite, and a splendid Cosmati floor (13th c.). The frescos in the crypt date back to the 8th c.

S. Croce in Gerusalemme, Piazza di S. Croce in Gerusalemme (near the Porta Maggiore). Alas, rather neglected by the pilgrims, even though it is one of the seven classical pilgrimage churches. Built by the Emperor Constantine in memory of his mother, St Helena, for the safe keeping of the Holy Cross. After numerous rebuildings, nothing remains of the legendary original. The campanile is Romanesque; the church acquired its present Baroque appearance in 1743. There are fragments of the Holy Cross and other relics of the Cross in the reliquary chapel. The apse fresco (15th c.) depicts the discovery of the Holy Cross by St Helena (who visited the Holy Land in c. 327).

Domine Quo Vadis?, Via Appia Antica, stands, according to the pious legend, on the spot where Christ met the Apostle Peter, who was trying to flee the city to elude Nero's persecution. 'Quo vadis?' (Where goest thou?) Peter asked the man, and he answered that he was going to Rome to be crucified a second time. Filled with remorse, Peter turned about and met the death of a martyr.

Chiesa del Gesù, Piazza del Gesù, mother church of the Jesuit Order, built for Cardinal Alessandro Farnese by Giacomo da Vignola from 1568 (vaulting and façade by Giacomo della Porta after Vignola's death in 1573). One of the great preaching churches in which the Jesuits took the field against the Reformation.

S. Giovanni in Laterano, Piazza S. Giovanni in Laterano, was entirely rebuilt by Borromini in 1650 out of the debris of the original church; the Baroque façade was added by Antonio Galilei in 1734. The central bronze door is ancient, having been taken from the

Senate-house, the *Curia Julia* in the Forum, as rebuilt by Diocletian after the fire of AD 283. According to legend, the high altar covers the heads of the chief Apostles, Peter and Paul. Via the left transept you may enter the extensive monastery gardens and the 13th c. cloister, decorated with Cosmati-work by one of the Vassalletti.

SS. Giovanni e Paolo, Piazza SS. Giovanni e Paolo, on the Celio: see page 58.

S. Giovanni a Porta Latina, Via di Porta Latina, lies tucked away just under the ancient city wall. An Early Romanesque delight, with a fine campanile and frescos of the Hohenstaufen period (1138–1254), differentiated from the stiff Byzantine style by their lively expression.

S. Ignazio, Piazza S. Ignazio, off the Via del Corso. Built in connection with the canonisation of St Ignatius Loyola (1622) as Rome's second large Jesuit church. The associated Jesuit College was begun at the same time. The church also contains the tomb of St Aloysius (Luigi Gonzaga), who entered the order at the age of seventeen and died of plague aged twenty-three (canonised 1726). The frescos by Andrea del Pozzo, especially that in the dome – a masterpiece of perspectival illusionistic painting, in which architecture and colours mingle with one another – are best seen from the circular marble plaque in the nave.

S. Lorenzo fuori le Mura, Piazza di S. Lorenzo: see page 71.

S. Luigi dei Francesi, Piazza S. Luigi dei Francesi, Via della Scrofa. This is the French national church. On the altar of the Contarelli Chapel (last on the left) is a masterpiece by Caravaggio, the second version of the *Inspiration of St Matthew* (1602/03). The first version was refused by the clergy because of its excessive realism and bought by Vincenzo Giustiniani. On the walls on either side of the chapel are two further examples of the dramatic, naturalistic power first introduced by Caravaggio into European painting.

S. Maria degli Angeli, Piazzale dell' Esedra (Piazza della Repubblica), was built into the *tepidarium* of the Baths of Diocletian by the then aged Michelangelo between 1563 and 1566, and altered by Luigi Vanvitelli (1700–73) from 1749. The vaulting is supported by eight ancient columns in red granite; the interior 'marble' decoration is entirely painted.

S. Maria dell'Anima, Via S. Maria dell'Anima, off the Piazza Navona, is the German (originally also the Dutch and Flemish) national church. Combining Gothic and Italian elements, it was built early in the 15th c. for the German fraternity by a German master mason. The tomb of Adrian VI (the last non-Italian pope before the present incumbent), to the right of the high altar, is by Baldassare Peruzzi. Next door is the former hospice and the present parish hall of the German community in Rome.

S. Maria in Aracoeli, on the Capitol, is supposed, according to legend, to stand on the spot where the Tiburtine Sibyl announced the birth of Jesus to the Emperor Augustus. The later Franciscan church (1250) was linked to the piazza below by means of a steep flight of 122 high steps, in thanksgiving for Rome's having escaped the plague of 1346. Do not miss the frescos by Pinturicchio in the first side-chapel to the right (c. 1485). The *Bambino Santissimo*, an infant Christ carved out of olivewood (brought by angelic despatch from the Garden of Gethsemane), is important to Romans: at one time, in cases of serious illness, it was brought round the houses in procession on a state carriage.

Santa Maria in Aracoeli

Numerous marble gravestones are built into the foundations. The Midnight Mass at Christmas is particularly solemn. Into the Dark Ages, the Senate of Rome met here and issued its resolutions.

S. Maria in Cosmedin, Piazza Bocca della Verità: see page 18.

S. Maria Maggiore, Piazza S. Maria Maggiore, one of the most important basilicas in terms of church and art history. An Early Christian foundation; the crib of Bethlehem was supposedly kept here. The occasion of its construction is also surrounded with legend. In 352, Pope Liberius and John the Senator both received at the same time from the Virgin, in a dream, the charge to erect a church on the hill in Rome where, next morning, they should find snow – and that on August 5th! On the Esquiline they found in midsummer snow fallen in the shape of a basilica. Hence the popular name of the church is even now *Santa Maria della Neve*. It was repeatedly rebuilt up to the 18th c. The apse contains the famous Jacopo Torriti mosaics (*Coronation of the Virgin*, 13th c.). The mosaics over the arch are 5th c.; earlier still are the scenes on the entablature of the nave.

S. Maria della Pace, Vicolo della Pace (near Piazza Navona), contains four frescos by Raphael (*Sibyls*), best visited early in the morning or Sundays

10.15–11.30 am. During the day the church is shut. Apply to the verger next door, in Bramante's cloister (1504).

S. Maria del Popolo, Piazza del Popolo, was remodelled by Bernini in the 17th c. The original church is supposed to have been built over Nero's grave, to exorcise the evil spirit. In the first side-chapel on the right is a marvellous fresco by Pinturicchio, the *Adoration of the Magi*; the Chigi chapel (second on the left) was designed by Raphael; to the left of the high altar are two famous Caravaggios. Martin Luther lived in the associated monastery during his stay in Rome (1510–11).

S. Maria della Vittoria, on the corner of Via XX Settembre and Via Bissolati, was built by Carlo Maderna (1608). Before the Second Vatican Council, this small church was one of the most flamboyantly over-furnished in all Rome – alas all now swept away. But it retains one of Bernini's masterpieces, the *Ecstasy of St Teresa* (central side-chapel on the left).

S. Maria in Trastevere, Piazza S. Maria in Trastevere: see page 19.

S. Maria sopra Minerva, behind the Pantheon, is the sole church in Rome wholly in the Gothic style, and built, according to legend, on the ruins of a temple of Minerva. It was rebuilt from 1280 by the Dominicans (with later unfortunate remodelling). The famous frescos by Filippino Lippi (1488–93) are in the Caraffa chapel in the right transept. Beneath the high altar is the headless body of St Catherine of Siena (the head is kept in Siena). The *Christ with the Cross*, to the left of the high altar, was left unfinished by Michelangelo.

S. Onofrio, Piazzale di S. Onofrio: see page 55.

S. Paolo fuori le Mura, Via Ostiense: see page 70.

St Peter's: see page 50.

S. Pietro in Vincoli, Piazza S. Pietro in Vincoli, near the Baths of Trajan on the Oppio, takes its name from the holy fetters with which St Peter was chained and which have been kept in the church since 439. The present building dates from the 15th c. Michelangelo's mighty *Moses* was supposed to have been part of the decoration of the tomb of Pope Julius II which was never completed.

Frescos by Filippino Lippi in Santa Maria sopra Minerva

S. Prassede, Via di S. Prassede, by S. Maria Maggiore: see page 57.

S. Prisca, Via di S. Prisca, on the Aventine, was built in the 6th c. over the house of the converted Jews Aquila and Prisca, mentioned in Paul's *Epistle to the Romans*, 16.3–4. The present appearance of the church derives from the 17th c. A temple of Mithras with very important frescos (c. AD 200–20) was discovered beneath the church. St Peter is supposed to have used the Doric capital kept in the church when he baptised Prisca.

S. Pudenziana, Via Urbana: see page 57.

SS. Quattro Coronati, Via dei SS. Quattro Coronati, near S. Clemente: see page 18.

S. Sabina, Piazza Pietro d'Illiria, on the Aventine: see page 18.

S. Sebastiano ad catacumbas, Via Appia Antica, beyond the Catacombs of St Callistus. One of Rome's seven pilgrimage churches. Completely rebuilt in the 17th c., but in all probability built originally in the 4th c. on the site of an Early Christian cemetery. Of the original church, only six columns remain. A stone is preserved here on which one can behold 'Christ's footprint'. The most famous catacombs of Rome are 13 m below the floor of this church. Some of these Roman tombs (which are not all Christian) are richly decorated with frescos and reliefs in stucco. The barrel vaults hacked out of the rock were originally to hold containers for ashes, but later entire rooms were cut into the side walls for inhumation burials. There are four floors dug into the tufa, and some Christian wall-paintings are preserved. The bones of St Sebastian are kept in a simple stone coffin in the crypt of the church.

S. Silvestro in Capite, Piazza di S. Silvestro, not far from the Trevi Fountain, is the national church of the English and Irish. It originates from the 8th c. and was rebuilt in its present form in 1690. The head post office of Rome, which stands beside it, occupies the former monastery and cloisters.

S. Stefano Rotondo, Via di S. Stefano Rotondo on the Celio, is a round church of the 5th c. whose rotunda is carried on twenty-two Ionic columns. The monument of King Stephen I of Hungary (canonised 1083) was decorated by Antonio Tempesta. The walls of the church carry frescos by Cristoforo Roncalli, 'il Pomarancio' (16th c.), which have been described as 'vacuous Mannerism'. See also page 58.

S. Trinità dei Monti, Piazza della Trinità dei Monti, at the top of the Spanish Steps, is a French foundation which was destroyed during the Napoleonic occupation and rebuilt by Louis XVIII. It belongs to the attached Convent of the Sacred Heart. Note the *Deposition* by Daniele da Volterra (second chapel on the left).

S. Paolo fuori le Mura, on the Via Ostiense, is no longer *fuori le Mura*, outside the city. The basilica's exposed situation has brought it a good deal of woe in former times. It was sacked by the Saracens, who landed at Ostia, and was burned almost to the ground in 1823, when a roof-worker left behind a brazier with live coals that he had been using. When the church had been rebuilt, an explosion in a nearby munitions factory blew out all the windows. Until the rebuilding of St Peter's, S. Paolo (built over the tomb of St Paul) was the biggest church in the world. It is one of the famous seven pilgrimage churches of Rome, visited at one time on foot but now by bus. (The others are S. Giovanni in Laterano, St Peter's, S. Maria Maggiore, S. Croce in Gerusalemme, S. Sebastiano ad catacumbas

S. Paolo fuori le Mura

and S. Lorenzo fuori le Mura.) The rebuilding followed the original ground-plan, but only a couple of fragments of the original construction now remain. However, it is worth viewing the cloister, which is the best-preserved in Rome (c. 1200–41), and, in the abbey's small museum, one or two treasures such as the bible of Charles the Bald with Ottonian illuminations, and an 11th c. bronze door chased with silver, which once formed the main west entrance of the church.

S. Agnese fuori le Mura is also some way from the centre, off the Via Nomentana. The young martyr Agnes, the granddaughter of the Emperor Constantine, is buried here. You can easily spend half a day visiting the basilica (originally 4th c.) and the buildings round it: the *Mausoleum of the two Constantias*, daughters of Constantine by different mothers, and the well-preserved catacombs. In the apse is a 7th c. mosaic. On January 21st, the feast-day of St Agnes, two lambs are consecrated over her tomb, and sacred vestments, which the Pope employs as gifts, made from their wool. In 1855 Pope Pius IX

and his entire retinue fell into the crypt below when the floor gave way, but no one came to any harm. The scene is depicted in a wall-painting.

S. Lorenzo fuori le Mura (on the Via Tiburtina, beyond the Termini Station), another of the pilgrimage churches, was destroyed by Allied bombing on July 19th 1943. An exact replica, including the cloister, has since been built; the bishop's throne, by Peter Vassalletto or his grandson, is however original (c. 1250). On the walls of the neighbouring cemetery, *Campo Verano*, one can still see numerous votive plaques, dedicated in front of a statue of the Virgin by poor local families in need.

The air-raid took the Romans completely by surprise, since no one believed it possible that the city of the popes might be bombed. The Pope (Pius XII) hurried to the scene, quicker than the King or Mussolini, who were jeered at while the Pope was cheered. Perhaps this air-raid was one of the impulses towards the subsequent dismissal of Mussolini (on July 24th–25th) and the Italian attempt to withdraw from the war.

Shopping

Antiquarian and secondhand bookshops in Rome are ideal places to find little presents or souvenirs. The most important are: *Rappaport*, 23 Via Sistina; *Querzola*, 23 Via del Babuino; *Libreria Antiquaria Roma*, 15 Via di Propaganda; *Cascianelli*, 15 Largo Febo. *Prints and drawings* are to be found at *Fabrizio Apolloni*, 148 Via del Babuino, especially the entire run of the popular Roman scenes of Bartolomeo Pinelli (19th c.); also on the stalls of the Largo della Fontanella di Borghese.

Bookshops: in the past few years, numerous bookshops have appeared in Rome and have often become meeting places for cultivated circles. One of these is the *Libreria Rizzoli*, 76 Via Veneto, open every evening till midnight. There they stock a very large selection of paperbacks in every language. The other branch of Rizzoli is at 15 Largo Chigi (near the Trevi Fountain) and has extended itself into a vast warehouse for books (ground floor and basement). It is extremely difficult to find an assistant to give you advice. You serve yourself and march to the cash-desk.

In the Piazza S. Silvestro is the *Remainders Bookshop*, where with a bit of specialist knowledge you can find marvellous bargains – all at half price. The reader with abstruse requirements is advised to try the *Libreria Tombolini*, Via IV Novembre: there you will find what is absent from all the other Roman bookshops, specialist advice and a very rich selection too of scholarly books. That was why the bookworm Palmiro Togliatti, the former leader of the Communist Party, was a regular customer. For leftist reading, however, there are two highly competent bookshops: *Libreria Rinascita* on the ground floor of the PCI building, 1–2 Via delle Botteghe Oscure, and *Libreria Feltrinelli*, 41 Via del Babuino. In the Libreria Rinascita you can also provide yourself with revolutionary and folk-music records (old and new).

At Feltrinelli's, there are so many revolutionary journals that it is hard to squeeze through the door. The back rooms of the extensive shop are a rendezvous for students. Without buying a thing, you can stand for hours, reading or browsing. The *Libreria Modernissima*, 43 Via della Mercede, also has an embarrassment of books, that are almost out over the street. On the table by the cash desk you will always find a display of the latest books.

Candied violets: *Moriondo e Gariglio*, 416 Via del Corso.

Cheeses: *Pascucci*, 44 Via Uffici del Vicario.

Children's clothes from 1–12 years, and pregnancy wear: there are two specialist shops in the Via Frattina, *La Cicogna* and *Prémaman*. Since the Romans spoil their children terribly and nothing is too good for them, delightful new designs come out all the time – and are very suitable as gifts.

[**Babysitters** can be obtained through *La Cicogna*, 138 Via Frattina, tel. 679 1912 (if necessary, English-speaking).]

Children's clothes from 2–16 are the speciality of *Tablo*, 96 Piazza di Spagna, and its branch at 84 Via della Croce. You can find there miniature versions of everything that elegant adults are wearing. Not cheap, but the clothes are of better quality than anywhere else in Rome – except at Schostal.

China and kitchenware, from a simple pot-lid through coffee-machines to fine collectors' items, at *Limentani*, 47 Portico d'Ottavia.

Cigarettes, matches, stamps and salt are in Italy bought not in shops or restaurants but in the State-

Shopping in the Via Frattina

owned kiosks, *Tabacchi*, which are marked with a big letter T.

Gifts are to be found in the numerous branches of *Standa*, whose large signs can be seen everywhere. A little dearer is *Rinascente*, the department store at the corner of *Via del Corso* and *Via del Tritone*. Four floors full of clothes, leather goods and attractive things for the house.

Italian toys may be bought at one or two specialist shops:

De Sanctis, 94 Via Veneto;

Federici & Mondini, 100 Via Totte Vecchia;

Galleria del 48, 100–105 Via di Pretis;

I Balocchi, Via Gregorio VII;

Zingone, Via della Maddalena.

Italian charcuterie: *Colantoni*, 14 Piazza Alessandria (made on the premises; but alas, few countries will permit the import of 'foreign' meats).

Italian roasted coffee: *La Tazza d'Oro*, 86 Via degli Orfani; *Caffè Sant' Eustachio*, 82 Piazza S. Eustachio.

Jewellery is not likely to be bought at *Bulgari* in Via Condotti, the most renowned and expensive shop in Rome, but, at least, do not fail to look over the vast display, with its really fine pieces. Not far away, at 6 Via Condotti, is the dependable *Silvio Ferrara*, where you can find an excellent choice of old jewellery. There are other, not quite so expensive shops in the streets off the Via Condotti.

Marrons glacés: *Giuliano*, 67 Via Paolo Emilio.

Modern art may be admired and bought in the following private galleries:

Il Segno, 4 Via Capo le Case, tel. 679 1387;

La Borgognona, 525 Via del Corso, tel. 361 0258;

La Medusa, 124 Via del Babuino, tel. 679 6546;

La Nuova Pesa, 46 Via del Vantaggio, tel. 65 2061;

Galleria Marlborough, 5 Via Gregoriana, tel. 678 4678;

Toninelli, 86 Piazza di Spagna, tel. 679 3488.

Pipes: in the little shop of *Carmignani* Bros, 40 Via della Colonna Antonina, you may buy the best pipes in the world, including the best Italian make, Castello.

Pullovers and cardigans are best and most cheaply bought in one of the numerous shops in Via del Gambero, which compete fiercely with one another.

Records: if you want new Italian records, you may confidently go to *Discoteca Frattina* in Via Frattina or to *Consorti* in Via Giulio Cesare.

Shoes: if you have sore feet from walking in Rome and simply must have some very comfortable shoes, try one of the shops in the neighbourhood of S. Maria sopra Minerva, such as *Tanfani*. These shops specialise in outfitting clergymen and nuns. Not merely shoes, but underclothes and woollen goods are of the highest quality, and not expensive.

Nowhere are shoes cheaper than in Rome, since the city has far too many shoeshops. You will find an enormous selection at *Sore*, a shop directly opposite the Trevi Fountain where one can buy in particular cheap versions of the latest models.

Stationery: you can find pretty things in paper and card, little boxes, trays and coasters at *Vertecchi* in Via Frattina and Via della Croce.

Ties: there is no point in paying the earth for smart silk ties when there are all those little shops in the *Via Frattina* selling off thousands of different designs at quite reasonable prices.

Underclothes, hose, scarves, woollen shawls are for good reason bought by Romans only at *Schostal* on Via del Corso, a long-established shop which combines the best quality with honest prices.

Wines: at *Chiarotti*, 7 Piazza Martiri di Belfiore; *Antiquariato Vini Italiani*, 7a Viale Liegi; *Enoteca Capranica*, 99 Piazza Capranica; *Placidi*, 76a Via della Croce; *Corsi*, 88 Via del Gesù.

Wines and liqueurs from the various **abbeys** and **monasteries** that still produce their own specialities: *Nardi*, 72 Corso Rinascimento.

Hours of business

Hours of business in Rome have

Street artists, Piazza Navona

become much shorter: shops open at 9 am and shut at 7 pm. If there is a break in the middle of the day, it lasts from 1–4 pm. But everyone pleases himself. All shops bar food shops are shut on Monday mornings. Food shops are correspondingly closed on Thursday afternoons. Many restaurants in Rome take Sunday as their obligatory rest day, and for that reason all restaurants in country areas are then open.

Food and drink

A reliable observer, Francesco Simoncini, has established that food in Rome has deteriorated markedly over the last five years in the face of mass tourism. Anyone who is in Rome for a good while, or fairly often, should certainly obtain a copy of the latest edition of his book, *Guida ai Ristoranti di Roma* (Sugar Editore), which can be found in all large bookshops. Here you have to hand an exhaustive catalogue, with exact classification, of all places to eat in Rome and its environs. There are also plenty of tips about what to avoid, such as the new fashion for making spaghetti with whisky, or risotto with champagne. The author also warns one to be wary of dishes made of minced meat, such as *polpette* or *bauletti*, and of *macedonia di frutta* (fruit salad). According to him, the gourmet ought only to order *bollito misto* (assorted cuts of boiled meat) at lunchtime. And he says plainly that one can only trust one's own judgement about whether the wine is decent or not. It is a common thing in Rome for the best wine to be served in the shabbiest eating places. Simoncini also remarks how fundamental it is in Rome to get on well with the waiter, for 'a waiter in Rome is no robot, who treats everyone the same, but an important and self-confident man, especially when he has been long in his profession.'

La Guida dell' Espresso, which awards stars, is always up-to-date. It can be found in any bookshop.

First-class restaurants

(with reference to the food, not necessarily the price):

Alfredo all' Augusteo, 30 Piazza Augusto Imperatore, tel. 678 1072

Carmelo alla Rosetta, 9 Via della Rosetta, tel. 656 1002

Chez Albert, 11 Vicolo della Vaccarella, tel. 656 5549

Nino, 11 Via Borgognona, tel. 679 5676

Taverna Antonina (Da Battaglia), 48 Via Colonna Antonina, tel. 678 3717

Papa Giovanni, 4 Via dei Sedari, tel. 656 5308

La Giada, 137 Via IV Novembre (first floor), tel. 679 8334

Cannavota, Piazza S. Giovanni in Laterano, tel. 77 5007

Ranieri, 26 Via Mario de' Fiori, tel. 679 1592

Dal Bolognese, 1 Piazza del Popolo, tel. 361 1426

Osteria Sant'Ana, 68 Via della Penna, tel. 361 0291

La Fontanella, 86 Largo Fontanella Borghese, tel. 678 3849

El Toula, 29b Via Lupa, tel. 687 3498

Margutta-Vegetariano, 119 Via Margutta, tel. 678 6033

Alfredo alla Scrofa, 104 Via della Scrofa, tel. 654 0163

Hosteria dell'Orso, 25 Via dei Soldati, tel. 656 4250

31 Al Vicario, 31 Via Uffici del Vicario, tel. 678 2500

Il Buco, 8 Via S. Ignazio, tel. 679 3298

Il Barroccio Er Faciolaro, 13 Via dei Pastini, tel. 678 3896

Hotel Massimo d'Azeglio, 14 Via Cavour, tel. 475 4101

Taverna Flavia, 9 Via Flavia, tel. 474 5214

Il Tinello, 16b Via di Porta Pinciana, tel. 48 6847

Girarrosto Toscano, 29 Via Campania, tel. 49 3759

St Andrews, 22 Via Lazio, tel. 474 5832

Harry's Bar, 150 Via Veneto, tel. 474 5832

George's, 7 Via Marche, tel. 48 4575

Sans Souci, 20 Via Sicilia, tel. 49 3504

Francesco Perilli, 53 Via Piemonti, tel. 46 4626

Giggi Fazzi, 22 Via Lucullo, tel. 46 4045

Ulpia, 2 Foro Traiano, tel. 679 6271

Roof-garden, Hotel Forum, 25 Via Tor de' Conti, tel. 679 2446

Passetto, 14 Via Zanardelli, tel. 687 9937

Ai Tre Scalini, 30 Piazza Navona, tel. 687 9148

Il Pianeta Terra, 94 Via Arco del Monte, tel. 656 9893

Il Cavaliere, 39 Via Banchi Nuovi, tel. 56 5776

Sabatini, 18 Vicolo S. Maria in Trastevere, tel. 581 8307

Cecilia Metella, 125 Via Appia Antica, tel. 513 6743

La Villa dei Cesari, 164 Via Ardeatina, tel. 513 6741

Good and relatively cheap

Mario, 56 Via della Vite, tel. 678 3818

Umberto al 34, 34 Via Mario de' Fiori, tel. 679 5091

Otello alla Concordia, 81 Via della Croce, tel. 679 1179

Fiaschetteria Beltramme, 39 Via della Croce

Della Campanella, 18 Vicolo della Campanella, tel. 687 5273

La Pentola, 120 Piazza Firenze, tel. 654 2607

La Matricianella, 4 Via del Leone, tel. 687 6205

Cesarina, 109 Via Piemonte, tel. 46 0828

Settimo, 14 Via delle Colonelle, tel. 678 9651

Da Gino, 85 Via Lugaretta, tel. 580 3403

L'Aquila, 138 Via Rasella, tel. 46 1214

Da Cesare alla Stamperia, 71 Via della Stamperia, tel. 678 3459

La Matriciana, 40 Via Viminale, tel. 46 1775

Da Tullio, 26 Via N. da Tolentino

La Pentolaccia, 9 Via Flavia, tel. 48 5777

Vecchia Roma, 18 Piazza Campitelli

Angelino a Tor Margana, 37 Piazza Margana, tel. 678 3328

Angelino ai Fori, 40 Largo Corrado Ricci, tel. 679 1121

Al Gladiatore, 5 Piazza del Colosseo, tel. 73 6276

Da Giggetto, 21 Via del Portico d'Ottavia, tel. 656 1105

Da Piperno a Monte Cenci, 9 Via Monte dei Cenci, tel. 686 1113

La Scuderia, 83 Via di Panico

Panzironi, 73 Piazza Navona

Maestrostefano, 88 Piazza Navona

La Carbonara, 23 Campo de' Fiori

Al Pallaro, 13 Largo del Pallaro

Romolo, 8 Via di Porta Settimia

Antica Pesa, 18 Via Garibaldi

Checco Er Carrettiere, 10 Via Benedetta

Mario's, 53 Via del Moro

Da Gino, 85 Via della Lungaretta

Al Pastarellaro, 33 Via S. Crisogono

Dalla Sora Lella, Isola Tiberina, 16 Via Ponte Quattro Capi

Il Comparone, 47 Piazza in Piscinula

Da Meo Patacca, 30 Piazza dei Mercanti

Da Fieramosca Ar Fosso, 3 Piazza dei Mercanti

Ai Trenini Er Montarozzo, 6 Via Appia Antica

Ices

The best ices are to be found at:

Giolitti al Vicario, 40 Via Uffici del Vicario

Pignotti, 103 Via Cola di Rienzo

Fassi, 45 Corso d'Italia

Tre Scalini, 28 Piazza Navona

Rosati, 25 Piazzale Clodio (the bar of the Italian TV company RAI-TV, open till midnight)

Espresso

The best espresso is to be found at:

Caffè Sant'Eustachio, 82 Piazza S. Eustachio

La Tazza d'Oro, 86 Via degli Orfani

Alemagna, 181 Via del Corso

Pizza

The best pizza is to be found at:

Pizzeria San Marco, 29 Via Tacito

La Capricciosa, 8 Largo dei Lombardi

Ristorante la Fiorentina, 24 Via Andrea Doria

Pizzeria Rustica, 45 Campo Marzio

Canepa, 84 Via V. E. Orlando

L'Augusteo, 5 Via della Frezza

La Berninetta, 57 Via Belsiana

Toto alle Carrozze, 9 Via delle Carrozze

Al Re degli Amici, 33b Via della Croce

La Matricianella, 4 Via del Leone

Il Barroccio Er Faciolaro, 13 Via dei Pastini

La Sagrestia, 89 Via del Seminario

Le Cave di Sant'Ignazio, 169 Piazza Sant'Ignazio

Pisciapiano Gioia Mia, 34 Via degli Avignonesi

Petrini, 23 Via Florida

Domiziano, 88 Piazza Navona

Pancrazio Al Biscione, 92 Piazza del Biscione

Il Pozzetto, 167 Borgo Pio
Taverna Cestia, Via della Piramide
Cestia

Nightspots

The following nightspots are recommended in winter:
Bagaglino (Cabaret), 75 Via Due Macelli, tel. 679 1439;
Cabala, 93 Via Monte Brianzo, tel. 46 3370;
Capriccio, 38 Via Liguria, tel. 474 4587;
Lo Scarabocchio, 8c Piazza Ponziani, tel. 580 0495;
Number One, 2 Via Lucullo, tel. 46 4576;
Oliviero Club 84, 84 Via Emilia, tel. 474 2205.

In summer it is worth going 12 km out on the Via Aurelia, to *Brigadoon*, tel. 690 0009, where you can dance in the open air.

Still farther away from Rome (30 km) is *Helio Cabala*, a very popular nightspot in Marino, in the Alban Hills: Via Spinabella, Marino, tel. 93 8225.

Holy Week celebrations in St Peter's

☆ Festivals and events

Of special interest are of course Easter and Christmas. On Easter Sunday an enormous crowd gathers in St Peter's Square to await the Pope's blessing *urbi et orbi* (to the City of Rome and to the world), which is bestowed after the solemn Mass from the central balcony of St Peter's. The Easter festivities begin however the previous Sunday, Palm Sunday, when children and country folk bring cleverly twisted stars, crosses and other shapes made of palm leaves and olive-twigs, which are hung up all year round in the house after being blessed. During Holy Week, you can still listen to the Gregorian chant of the Benedictines in S. Anselmo on the Aventine. The eternal flame is relighted in the basilicas on Easter Saturday.

At Christmas, Midnight Mass is especially splendidly celebrated at S. Maria in Aracoeli, S. Maria Maggiore and S. Anselmo. In many churches, the nativity cribs, many with Counter-Reformation figures, remain in place long after Epiphany. The best-known cribs are to be found in S. Maria in Aracoeli, S. Marcello, S. Maria in Via and S. Carlo alle Quattro Fontane. The biggest can be seen all year round, in SS. Cosma e Damiano.

On January 21st, young lambs are consecrated in S. Agnese fuori le Mura. A Mass in honour of the popular Roman saint, Philip Neri (1515–95, canonised 1622), is celebrated on March 16th in the private chapel of the Palazzo Massimo alle Colonne.

The festival of the *Madonna della Neve* is celebrated on August 5th in the basilica of S. Maria Maggiore; white flowers are distributed in memory of the miracle of the snowfall which led to the basilica being built. On January 1st, in the Catacomb of St Priscilla on the Via Salaria, there is a solemn procession in honour of the martyrs, with lanterns and litanies.

Beyond the city: selected excursions

Rome is ringed with worthwhile places to visit.

West: You quickly reach the sea, either the little fishing village of *Fiumicino* or *Ostia-Lido*, nowadays a big, dreary town of 80,000 inhabitants. At one time, *Ostia Antica* and the smaller archaeological site of *Porto* lay on the sea.

North: Full of Etruscan sites and cemeteries, such as *Cerveteri, Tarquinia, Città Castellana, Veii, Vetralla, Barbarano Romano, Blera. Viterbo* is medieval. The port of *Civitavecchia* has the mighty fortress *Forte Michelangelo* to offer, which was begun from Bramante's design and completed by Michelangelo.

South: Here the *Castelli Romani* beckon: the Pope's summer residence at *Castel Gandolfo*, the wine area of *Frascati, Monteporzio* and *Marino* – the highest summit of the Alban Hills, *Monte Cavo* (900 m), can comfortably be walked – and the two volcanic lakes, Lake *Albano* and Lake *Nemi*, side by side. From here, the coast road (207) leads on to *Anzio* and *Nettuno*, past *Monte Circeo* and *Terracina* to picturesque *Sperlonga* and finally *Naples*.

East: In this direction lie *Tivoli, Palombara Sabina* (near *Monte Gennaro*, with its marvellous views, which can be reached by gondola lift), the monastery town *Subiaco* and many other places tucked away in the hills, where an almost medieval way of life has survived. By taking the new motorway (A24), you can reach the remarkable town of *L'Aquila* in the Abruzzi, with its numerous churches, in an hour and a half.

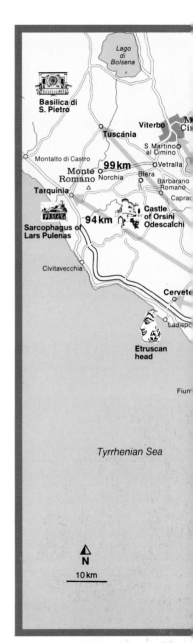

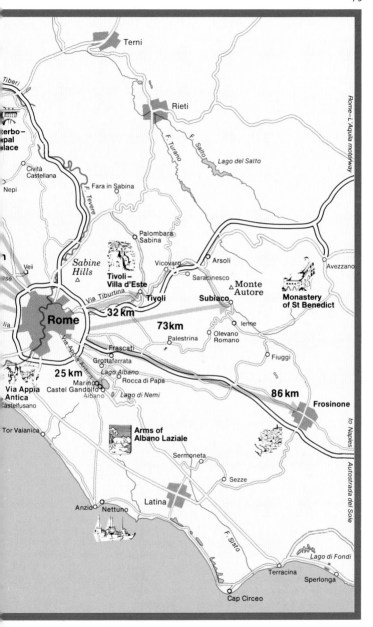

The mysterious Etruscans

In Rome it is inevitable that one will quickly develop a passion for Antiquity, and in particular an interest in Etruscan remains. This can be satisfied by admiring Etruscan art (in the Villa Giulia and the Vatican collections). But not merely that way: it is above all the combination of art and landscape offered by these excursions to southern Etruria that will attract one to the surviving remains of this highly cultivated people, which once ruled Rome and later was crushed and Latinised.

There are so many possibilities that any suggestions have an air of arbitrariness. One can get to dozens of Etruscan cemeteries equally well by train (on the *Viterbo* line), by bus (A.CO.TRAL, tel. 5 7531) or by car. For one thing must be emphasised: we can now only get an impression of the Etruscans from their treatment of the dead, from their almost cheerful funerary customs, directed towards a happy existence in the world hereafter. In the Villa Giulia is a famous terracotta sarcophagus with a happy-looking married couple on the top, half-reclining and gazing out at us as though death really had lost all its sting.

Cerveteri

The *necropolis of Cerveteri* (44 km from Rome down the *Via Aurelia*) is our first goal and most important witness. The settlement itself goes back to the 8th c. BC. The high point of Etruscan power came in the late 7th–6th c. when, after the collapse of the Etruscan monarchies, loosely allied bands of warriors from all the heartland cities expanded southwards, conquering much of Latium and eventually Campania, and later also northwards, into the Po Valley. But they were checked in the 5th c. BC by the Greeks in the south and from 400 BC by the Celts in the north. Rome completed the process in a series of intermittent wars over two centuries from 435 BC: by 241 BC all of Etruria was in her hands. Today Cerveteri lives (apart from by agriculture) off its neighbouring necropolis, now excavated, whose great tufa *tholoi* are smothered in flowers and bay-trees.

The deep-dug chambers of these aristocratic graves did not only contain what can be seen now, the couches for the dead carved into the tufa, and the wall-paintings of hunting, warfare and domestic life. Already in the medieval period, utensils of gold and bronze were being taken, and even today there is an entire army of grave-robbers who surreptitiously extract pottery and other remains and sell them for a great profit. Some of what the archaeologists have found can be seen in the small new museum, organised in an exemplary fashion, in the *Orsini* castle (in the centre of the present town). The plans and photographs, including aerial shots, make clear that over a wide area the ground is honeycombed with thousands of subterranean, overgrown tombs.

Tarquinia, Blera, Norchia

The *Via Aurelia* takes you, a little inland from the coast where the now excavated port of Pyrgi was situated, to *Tarquinia* (92 km from Rome). In the museum there you can see the finest examples of Etruscan painting, and, escorted by trained guides, you can walk out over the fields to the entrances of a number of famous tombs.

But if you want to penetrate more deeply into the Etruscan achievement, you need to drive along the side-roads in the *Campagna*, which looks flat and monotonous but is constantly scored by wild chasms in the tufa and by narrow, overgrown watercourses. The Etruscans, like their ancestors the Villanovans, always built their settlements on inaccessible outcrops, and buried their dead in chambers hollowed out in the soft, brown stone of the rocky walls. Their cities have disappeared, or lie beneath modern settlements, but their tombs are still there, used as cowsheds, as barns or as wine-cellars.

You can push on down the *Via Aurelia* as far as *Montalto di Castro*, and strike inland along the 312 a little way to reach the complete, delicate Etruscan bridge (*Ponte dell'Abbadia*) in front of the castle of *Canino* (where there is an attractive museum with the treasures found in nearby *Vulci*). Less far is the trip inland from Tarquinia along the 1 *bis* via *Monte Romano* to the Etruscan valleys of *Barbarano*, *Blera* and *Norchia*. Vehicular roads carry one to a certain point, but the secrets of the rock tombs can be explored only on foot. The late King Gustav VI of Sweden financed excavations here and took part in them himself. Wherever you go in this region – *Sutri*, *Nepi*, *Castel Sant'Elia*, *Cività Castellana* (ancient *Falerii*) – the haunting Etruscan past goes with you.

Viterbo

The town of Viterbo is probably an Etruscan foundation, but more than anything else it is an incomparable medieval town. You need do no more than look at the famous 13th c. *Papal Palace* or wander through the gloomy quarter of *S. Pellegrino* to imagine the cruelties of time past, from which the pilgrims of old, travelling down the 'Road of the Franks', sought refuge and rest behind the walls of Viterbo. How cheerful and idyllic by contrast is the countryside round about: the woods covering *Monte Cimino* (1,053 m), the Cistercian abbey of *S. Martino al Cimino* (from where one can see the sea), the three lakes of *North Latium* (Lakes *Bolsena*, *di Vico*

and *Bracciano*). Despite their volcanic origin, these crater lakes are quite lovely and still unspoilt. Will they remain so? The preservationists are struggling hard to save them from speculative builders. In North Latium, or rather 'Southern Etruria', Rome still today has a paradise that has lasted for millennia.

Palestrina and the Praenestine and Sabine Hills

If you escape from Rome early in the morning into the hills round Palestrina, you will find the *Via Prenestina* (Porta Maggiore) a narrow and unpleasant exit road; but you have the advantage of driving the other way from the commuter traffic, which is all going into Rome. Buses to Palestrina leave from the Termini Station.

Palestrina

The first destination is Palestrina, ancient *Praeneste* (c. 40 km), once one of the most important towns of Latium. From a distance it looks picturesque enough, clinging to the steep rock face, but from nearer quite poor, still showing damage from the War. Music-lovers will recall that *Palestrina* (c. 1525–94), for many years the director of the *Cappella Giulia* in Rome, was born here.

You should aim for the commanding heights above the town, the upper part of the gigantic terraced sanctuary of *Fortuna Primigenia*, begun after c. 150 BC. It was the bomb damage in 1944 which provided the impetus to excavate the remains systematically and to turn the 17th c. baronial palace of the *Barberini* and *Colonna* families, which occupies the apex of the temple, into one of Italy's finest museums.

Walking through this combination of Antique remains and Early Modern princely architecture is a double pleasure: a museum that constantly lures the delighted visitor to gaze out of one of the enormous casements at the majestic view down to the plain below. You stand, as the historians of religion say, on numinous ground: the vast sanctuary was from time immemorial the site of the oracle of Fortuna Primigenia, the 'goddess of fortune, first-born (of Jupiter)'. She was originally associated with the well-being of mothers and children, but the temple owed its wealth and fame to the oracle. Oracles were given in the lower sanctuary (earlier than 192 BC), in the form of inscribed slips of oakwood which were tossed in the air by a boy, to land at random. The resulting messages were then interpreted by experts. As well as a cult centre Praeneste became a popular summer resort.

Olevano Romano

From Palestrina, the road (155) takes us on 8 km to the turn-off to Olevano Romano. Here we encounter a quite different *genius loci*. This little medieval hilltop town (once the feudal property of the Borghese family) so fired the Romantic imagination of German painters in the last century that they acquired two houses for artists, the *Villa Serpentara* ('Serpents' Grove') and the *Casa Baldi*, which even now are available to German scholars and students. In the oak copse of Serpentara you can inspect stone medallion likenesses of some of these German-Romans. There is also a likeness of Kaiser Wilhelm II. Their brand of Romanticism is utterly remote to us, even if the landscape, with its olive-trees and vine trellises, and its old grey alleys and roofs, still makes an extremely attractive impression.

Round about Subiaco

You carry on up the narrow road through the hills for about 20 km, between bare, picturesque fells, to *Subiaco*. This spot on the upper reaches of the River Aniene (carried to Rome over four aqueducts) is redolent of the past. The importance of Subiaco lay in its water. The Emperor Nero caused three artificial lakes to be made, the *Simbruina stagna* (hence the Latin name *Sub laqueum* or *Sublaqueo*, 'below the lake'), as well as a large villa, which he linked to Rome by building the *Via Sublacensis*. Tacitus reports in the *Annals* that in AD 60 Nero was almost struck by lightning while at table here.

The town and castle are of less interest to us than the religious sites, which stand a little way off: you turn right off the road from Olevano just before the town. When St Benedict of Nursia withdrew here around 500, the imperial buildings were still intact. But the devout immigrant brought a crowd after him: twelve monasteries grew up in the well-watered valley, and the first Benedictine monastery was the seed of greater things, including the mighty Monte Cassino on the road to Naples. The monastic houses of St Benedict and his sister St Scolastica in Subiaco, the churches, cloisters and archives give us even today, with their richly painted frescos, the best insight into the spirit of early medieval anchoritism, even though later centuries, especially the Sienese School of the 14th c., have added layers of their own vision. In these places, masonry, rock and the irrepressible luxuriance of nature combine into a mysterious unity.

A motor road, which is however also suitable for walking, takes you from the Monastery of St Benedict and his holy cave (*Grotta Sacra*) to another cavern with a spring (*Grotta dell'Inferniglio*) and from there to the village of *Ienne*. You are now on the south-east slopes of the towering *Monte Autore*, the second highest peak in the *Monti Simbruini*, on a road which takes you via Vallepietra to the pilgrimage church of *S. Trinità*, 1,680 m above sea-level. On the first Sunday in May, an extremely colourful throng of pilgrims gathers here from the surrounding countryside, some by bus from towns, some by horse and donkey from the hill villages.

Getting into your convenient car again, take the road to *Arsoli*, a matter of 20 km. Here you must decide whether to take the fine new *Rome-L'Aquila* motorway and so reach Tivoli (exit *Man-dela*) quickly (the road does have fine views), or to go via *Vicovaro* on the ordinary road (5). In Vicovaro, a small side-road (to Licenza) leads to *Horace's farm* (9 km), ancient ruins hidden away in a very picturesque, verdant valley: a lovely walk, not in the least strenuous.

Tivoli

But if you need to conserve your ability to take things in, drive straight to *Tivoli*, cutting through the town via the serpentine valley road down to the *Emperor Hadrian's summer residence*, the *Villa Adriana*. The much travelled Emperor

Hadrian's Villa, Tivoli

Fountains in the Villa d'Este gardens, Tivoli

built this vast complex towards the end of his life (from AD 125), as a sort of compendium of all the buildings he had seen and admired in Egypt, Greece, etc. The past, underground, overgrown. stalks the impressive excavated remains of temples, lakes, baths and palaces. In the olive-groves you can feel the hollow ground under your feet. There is nothing more pleasurable than spending an early summer afternoon in the park under the cherry-laurels and chestnut-trees.

There is a great deal besides to see in Tivoli (ancient *Tibur*). But you have come to enjoy yourself, not to cover everything, and should hurry off to a restaurant back in Tivoli, in order to be able as a finale to visit the gardens of the

Villa d'Este, which are illuminated at night (from 9 pm). The palazzo itself (from 1550) is unassuming, and serves only as a gateway to the famous marvel of water-engineering beneath the lines of giant cypresses. The waters of the *River Aniene*, which fall into the valley in a high cascade just outside Tivoli, stimulated Cardinal Ippolito d'Este (and his heirs) to commission this unique series of fountains and waterfalls from the architects Pirro Ligorio and, later, Bramante.

Everywhere, in ever renewed sallies and falls, the jets of water cascade from hundreds of spouts, basins, runnels and steps. Nowhere does one grasp better than here that, in the Italian conception of nature, only the ornamental garden has value, the exorcism of nature's untamed luxuriance into a delimited realm of artifice. That is also true of the 'English Park' in the nearby *Villa Gregoriana*, by means of which Pope Gregory XVI in 1835 linked the waterfalls and rapids of the Aniene into a system, surmounted by the *Temple of Vesta*. It is scarcely surprising that Tivoli was a favourite subject for English painters and watercolourists from the late 18th c. – above all Turner, with his *Tivoli Sketchbook* (1820). (One may visit the Villa d'Este every day except Monday.)

On the homeward journey, do not miss the *Bagni di Tivoli* (Acque Albule) and the smell of its hot sulphur springs, whose therapeutic value, well known to the Romans, is still highly prized. Otherwise this is the edge of Rome in its least attractive aspect, an industrial area in complete disorder, in the process of being dismantled to move to Pomezia-Latina. 'Tourist Rome' begins again only once we get through the *Porta Pia*.

A day by the sea
Castelfusano

Rome has plenty of beaches but alas no inviting water to bathe in. By way of exception, the working class (the *popolino*) has a better deal than the well off. The working-class resort of *Castelfusano*, which former President Giuseppe Saragat set aside during his period of office (it belonged once to the House of Savoy, but by this time to the State), is Rome's best social achievement in decades. Over a mile of sand dunes south of Ostia-Lido, open dawn to dusk, free, (mostly) well looked after, provided with changing-cabins, and – most important of all – far enough away from the mouth of the polluted Tiber. To get to it without a car, take the B line on the metro from *Termini Station* or *Lido di Ostia Station*, which of course once out of town runs

on the surface through the Campagna. From the terminus, *Cristoforo Colombo*, buses go to the resort. It is a good idea, once again, to start early. For when the limited space is all taken up, the entrance gates are closed.

On this excursion, especially on a busy Sunday, you have the chance to observe Roman life at close quarters. There is Mother, who carries a complete midday meal for the entire family (say twelve people) in great bags or baskets: the inevitable spaghetti to start with, veal or pork cutlets, vegetables, salad, pudding and drinks, all piled onto folding tables, with sunshade or awning, which has been brought along too. The fussiness is half the point, and perhaps the real pleasure, of the family outing. The older generation is rather sceptical of the watery element, contenting itself with the fresh breeze. The younger generation has learned to splash about in the water, but the mothers frequently call out anxiously, as mother ducks do with their young.

Supposing that half a Sunday on the crowded sandy grill-pan suffices, at midday you could enjoy some fish, either in one of the small number of restaurants tucked away in the *Pineta* (pine wood) of Castelfusano, which has a heavenly scent of resin and is agreeably secluded and deserted, or, by driving across the town of Ostia, in the harbour of Fiumicino, where there is one fish restaurant after another all the way along the arm of the Tiber, which is canalised here before debouching into the sea. Summer and winter, Romans are fond of spending their Sundays in Fiumicino, with a walk along the mole, where the fishing smacks arrive in the early afternoon and unload and sell their catch, and where the luxury yachts of the wealthy bob in the brackish water of a little marina.

Ostia Antica

Ostia Antica

The afternoon is excellently suited to visiting *Ostia Antica* or the area of *Porto*, the harbours of imperial Rome. In Ostia Antica, the excavations have

Statue at Ostia Antica

brought more than sherds to light: an entire town, streets and all, with well-preserved (partly restored) apartment blocks, gives one the sense of what it was like to live there when it had 80,000 inhabitants (like modern Ostia-Lido). It was above all the grain needed to feed the population of the metropolis that made Ostia Antica the most important suburb of ancient Rome. Today we can still admire the Romans' intelligent solutions to the problems of urbanisation: drainage and heating systems, water supplies, cold-stores, bathing complexes, bakeries, fishponds, bathtubs, oil- and grain-stores, the merchant shipping facilities, temples, barracks, fountains, and a big theatre. If you are in luck (or have planned things well), there will be an open-air performance in the theatre, a Greek tragedy or a Roman comedy. And then it is worth eating supper in a restaurant near the medieval fortress in the village, outside the gates of the archaeological site. Even if you return home late after the theatre, there are still bus and train connections back to Rome.

Useful things to know

Rome, the city and its inhabitants

There is virtually no industry in Rome and no commerce: it is a passive place. But people couldn't manage without Rome, though the Milanese still claim that their city is the *capitale morale*, the capital as far as energy and public-spiritedness are concerned, and that Rome is merely the *capitale legale*, the capital according to the letter of the law.

During the period of the great national movement towards unification, the *Risorgimento*, before 1870, the people of Turin, the capital at that time, had similar reservations about Rome. Nevertheless the great statesman Cavour could not but declare Rome the future capital of Italy – and so the city was captured in 1870 and removed from papal control. At that time, Rome had not many more than 200,000 inhabitants.

Since then, immigrants from all over Italy have continually poured in; numerically, there are not many real Romans still around. But the Roman cast of mind has gradually spread to the newcomers. In fact, everything in Rome still happens at a more leisurely pace than in the industrial cities of the north or in tightly

'The Roman art of improvising'

administered cities like Florence or Bologna. Instead of industrial plants Rome has its vast machinery of administration, the government departments, the party headquarters, and the head offices of insurance companies, nationalised industries, banks and so on.

It is claimed that Rome today has 3.5 million inhabitants, but the exact number is not known. Most of these newcomers stem from the countryside around Rome, near or far – from Latium, from the Campagna, from southern Tuscany, from the Abruzzi. The flight from the land has primarily been directed towards the capital. The immigrants were of course not people who paid taxes but people generally in want of everything, work and somewhere to live. This has had the effect of finally producing an 'industry' in Rome: building speculation and feverish construction work, which however is halted as soon as there is an economic down-turn.

Nowadays the immigration has decreased; but for years there were annually on average 90,000 newcomers with hopes of finding work and shelter in Rome. As one can well imagine, this development has had the result of creating a vast municipal debt, and still it has proved impossible to provide enough schools, hospitals and all the other social infrastructure needed. The wild building speculation has also spoiled the appearance of the city. Only the historic centre is relatively unscathed, but it is choked by a cement-belt that goes on for miles. This unhealthy process continues even today: the apartment blocks push ever further out into the Campagna. Some ten years ago, a start was indeed made on splitting the city into different administrative units. But these local councils have only very slowly and laboriously begun to function, or even to make any sort of impression on the awareness of their inhabitants. The zoning plan which came into force in 1964 has been a dead letter, since the local authority has no money to buy the land which is supposed to serve communal purposes. The authorities have not coped with land poaching and have turned out to be entirely lacking in energy. As yet, no one has ever heard of an apartment block built without planning permission being pulled down again – so everyone does just what he likes.

In view of these facts, one must regard it as a considerable achievement that Rome does not simply collapse into chaos, and that the city council has succeeded despite everything at least in getting a bit of air into the centre and restoring the views of the noble sights of Rome. The Roman shopkeepers for long protested against the introduction of

A Roman carabiniere

the pedestrian zones – until they finally realised that they help rather than hinder shoppers. One fine day perhaps the Romans will also learn to leave their cars at home or at least use the underground car-parks. Then the buses too would run better. The inner city has already been appreciably relieved by the metro line A, brought into service in 1980.

Everyone, the tourist included, must in any case get used to how things are in Rome. The many thousand foreigners who live and work there become surprisingly rapidly accustomed to the chaos and up to a point seem to enjoy it. Of course that is partly because they keep Roman hours, and therefore have lots of free time and make frequent trips to the sea or into the Campagna.

Despite the saying that all roads lead to Rome, there is only one road which really meets modern standards, the *Autostrada del Sole*. The *Via Aurelia* is indeed dual carriageway when it approaches Rome, but until you reach Civitavecchia there are constant hold-ups, and there are no bypasses round any of the towns. That is also true of the other ordinary main roads, which mostly still follow the lines of the old Roman roads.

Rail journeys, whether from north or south, terminate with few exceptions at the *Termini Station*. Only for the immediate area are there other, smaller stations, such as *Stazione Trastevere* (Fiumicino, but also Pisa), *Tiburtina* (Terni), *Via Giovanni Giolitti* (Ciampino and the *Castelli Romani*), *Roma Nord Piazzale Flaminio* (Viterbo), etc.

All flights (except special flights for heads of state) leave from the *Aeroporto Leonardo da Vinci*, generally known as *Fiumicino*, from the small fishing village of that name nearby. A third runway was recently completed, but even that will not be sufficient for very long. The airport buildings are themselves too small for the rapidly increasing traffic.

That Rome actually has its own waterway to the sea, the lower reaches of the Tiber, has not so far been of any practical use. Apart from a few rowing crews, people do not travel on the Tiber. For a very long time now it has not been used for bathing, since it is probably one of the world's most polluted rivers. Unfortunately it poisons the sea for miles out – and the sewage works are even now not in full operation.

Despite being only 20 km from the sea, Rome has no sea-port. All this points to the fact that Rome is not a centre of production, not a place where there is a great volume of trade, but simply one single enormous consumer city.

Travel documents

No visa is required by British or US visitors staying under three months. British tourists need a valid standard passport or British Visitor's Passport.

Customs regulations

Luggage and objects of personal use can be brought into Italy free of customs duty. This includes: 2 cameras and 10 films, 1 video camera and 10 films, portable radio, portable musical instrument, portable tape-recorder, portable typewriter, telescope or binoculars. There is no duty on articles of no commercial value, such as food and souvenirs.

In addition EC residents may import and export (duty paid): 300 cigarettes or 75 cigars or 400 g tobacco; 1.5 litres of spirits over 22% (or 3 litres up to 22%) and 5 litres of wine; 1 kg coffee, 200 g tea, 75 g perfume.

The main duty-free allowances are: 1

The Colosseum from the Forum

litre of spirits over 22% (or 2 litres up to 22%) and 2 litres of wine; 200 cigarettes or 50 cigars or 250 g tobacco.

Non-EC visitors should check allowances with their travel agent.

Currency

At the moment legal tender consists of: coins of 5, 10, 20, 50, 100, 200 and 500 lire, and banknotes of 1,000, 2,000, 5,000, 10,000, 50,000 and 100,000 lire. The 50,000 and 100,000 lire notes are legal tender only in Italy, not abroad. In addition, the grooved telephone tokens (*gettoni*) are used as coins (200 lire).

You can obtain up to 300,000 lire with one Eurocheque.

You may carry as much foreign currency into Italy as you wish, though the amount taken out on leaving the country may not exceed the amount taken in. You may take as much Italian money into the country as you wish, and up to 500,000 lire out.

Exchange rates are published in the national press, or can be obtained from banks.

Bringing your car

Your ordinary insurance certificate provides you only with third-party insurance while you are abroad. It is advisable to bring an international 'green card' certificate with you, to avoid tedious discussions at police checks. It is obligatory to have, besides your registration documents and your driving licence, a nationality plate at the back, and a warning triangle. In addition, you must have a pack of spare bulbs for headlights, side-lights and indicators. Cars in Italy are regularly broken into for the sake of the radio: it is advisable to have either a removable set or a good anti-theft device. Never leave your car unlocked even for a few minutes.

For safety reasons it is forbidden to carry a can of spare fuel or to fill cans at petrol stations. Concessionary petrol coupons may be obtained from RAC offices (personal callers only) or when you cross the border.

Traffic conditions

Traffic in Rome is not as hectic as it was some years ago. The speed limit is 50 kph (31 mph), though it is of course not always observed. The 'slalom-driving' that used to be so popular, constantly weaving in and out of lanes to overtake, has died away with the increase in traffic. Still undiminished is the extraordinary trustfulness of the pedestrians, who launch themselves into the maelstrom looking neither left nor right. They are used to drivers keeping their eyes open for them. Damage to cars is common – if it is not serious, the owner often just shrugs his shoulders. Police reactions are quite unpredictable.

Hired cars

Hertz:
Central Booking Office, tel. 54 7991
Termini Station, tel. 474 0389
Hilton Hotel, tel. 34 3758
133 Viale America (EUR), tel. 591 5544
Airport (Fiumicino, international arrivals), tel. 60 1448
Avis:
1231 Via Tiburtina, tel. 409 0959/63
Maggiore Autonoleggio:
Central Booking Office, tel. 85 1620
8 Av Po, tel. 85 8698

57/58 Piazza della Repubblica, tel. 46 3715
Airport (Fiumicino, international arrivals), tel. 60 1678

Buses and metro

These are the chief means of transport in Rome. You can reach every corner of the city by municipal bus, and these also travel far out into the Campagna. The most practical way to find the bus routes is to buy a good map of Rome which marks them, such as the folding plan with street index published by Verdesi. The modern Line A of the metro links the eastern suburbs with the centre and the area of St Peter's Square. The old Line B connects Termini Station to the Colosseum, the EUR garden suburb, the south-west of the city and the beach at Ostia-Lido. The two lines interchange only at Termini Station. Metro tickets can be purchased at the machines in the metro stations, bus tickets in *tabacchi* marked with a T. Buy a book of ten or a weekly season ticket. There are no through-tickets. Bus-stops are marked by large yellow sign-boards bearing the numbers and main stops on the route. On most routes, the buses cease early in the evening; after that, they are replaced by night buses, but there are not many of them. It is advisable to put your hand out as the bus approaches. Practically all buses in the inner city have no conductor: you must clip your ticket (unless it is a season ticket) in one of the machines in the bus. When you wish to get off, give the bus-driver plenty of warning by pushing the button near the exit door. Roman bus-drivers are often spirited, especially when they have an empty stretch of road in front; and they like braking pretty hard. So hold on firmly, since you generally will not find a seat. Conductors and passengers willingly give information.

Young women sometimes find themselves the unwilling objects of male attention: a furious *'basta!'* generally helps.

Bus travel outside Rome

There is an extensive network of bus routes available for trips into the countryside around Rome. They depart relatively frequently and are extremely cheap.

Head Office of A.CO.TRAL. (the Roman Omnibus Company) is at 131 Via Ostiense, tel. 5 7531. There you can ask about current departure times and the different bus stations, which are distributed among different squares in the city.

Most important bus stations:
For Cerveteri, Bracciano, Tolfa, etc. (northern Latium): Lepanto metro-station.
For places along the Via Casilina (to Anagni, Frosinone): Piazza Castro Pretorio.
For Fiumicino and other places towards the sea: Via G. Giolitti (the long side of Termini Station).
For Ostia: Piazzale Ostiense (Stazione Lido Centro).
For Palestrina, Zagarolo, etc. along the Via Prenestina: Piazza del Cinquecento, in front of Termini Station.
For Tivoli: Piazza di Indipendenza (near Termini Station), Via Curtatone/Via Gaeta corner. Tickets from the office next to buses.

Taxis

Roman taxi-drivers are extremely forthcoming and talkative. Tariffs are still reasonable, which naturally suggests that one should be generous with the tip. In Rome, as elsewhere, taxis have the peculiarity of never being available when you want one most urgently.

Otherwise there are rows of them at cab-stands, where they have to return after each fare. It is actually forbidden to hail an empty taxi on the street: if you are in luck, the driver will stop all the same, but you can't count on it. The lack of taxis is most evident at Termini Station. If you arrive on an international train, you may have to wait an hour for a taxi. It is better to plunge straight into the bus system. You should not entrust yourself to the touts who whisper in your ear, *'Taxi, dove vuol andare?'*. At *Leonardo da Vinci* airport there are always enough taxis; the fare is around 50,000 lire. Each Roman taxi-driver must undertake airport-duty several times a year; it is unpopular because it is time-consuming and not worth while.

A few handy tips to end with. Travelling by taxi in Rome is not exorbitantly expensive. Travelling with one's own car is a nightmare, especially in the inner city, which is plastered with No Entry signs. There are big car-parks under the *Villa Borghese* and at the edge of the city, by the *Ponte Flaminio*. There you can *Park and Ride*, park your car and travel by bus all day, for only a few lire (very little used by the Romans!).

Post and telephone

Stamps (*francobolli*) are sold in post offices and in the tobacco-monopoly stands, *tabacchi*, marked with a large T outside. Use standard-sized envelopes for letters. There are public telephones in bars and shops which display the black and yellow sign *Telefono pubblico*. If they do not take ordinary coins, you can buy tokens for 200 lire apiece at the cash desk. But there are now many modern telephones that take coins (100 and 200 lire only) and phone cards (*carta telefonica*, also available from tabacchi). It is more expensive to telephone from a hotel, since there one has to pay a surcharge per unit.

To telephone abroad from Italy, first dial the international code (0044 for the UK, 01139 for the US and Canada), then the area code without the initial 0, then the subscriber's number.

The head telecommunications office (SIP) is in Via S. Maria in Via (just near the Trevi Fountain, not far from the head post office in Piazza S. Silvestro), and is open from 8 am till 9.45 pm.

Camping

There are the following campsites in Rome (the distance figures given in the list refer to the appropriate kilometre posts to look for):
A.I.C., 61 Viale Olimpiadi, tel. 396 4709
Campeggio Roma, km 8.1, Via Aurelia, tel. 622 3018
Camping Flaminio, km 8, Via Flaminia Nuova, tel. 327 9006
Camping Seven Hills, 1216 Via Cassia, tel. 376 5571
Pineta Arca, km 18, Via Cristoforo Colombo, tel. 606 5062
Club Méditerranée Italia, 136 Viale Europa, tel. 592 0287

Public holidays

New Year's Day; January 6th (Epiphany); Easter Sunday and Monday; April 25th (Liberation Day); May 1st (Labour Day); June 29th (only in Rome itself); August 15th (Ferragosto and Assumption); November 1st (All Saints' Day); December 8th (Immaculate Conception); December 25th and 26th (Christmas).

Electrical supply

In most hotels, the electric current is 110 or 220 volts; you can check by looking at the lightbulbs. English and American plugs (*spina*) do not fit in Italian sockets (*presa*). Even if the voltage is right, you need an adaptor (*adattore*), but they may be difficult to find, even in specialist shops. It is therefore advisable to buy a multi-purpose Continental adaptor before you leave home.

Tipping

This is expected by everyone for everything, and always gratefully received even when the tip is not large. Only the railway porters are hard to satisfy. Even the *maschere*, the young women who show you to your seats in the theatre or cinema, generally expect a small tip, as in France. For most services 10 to 15% is the norm. If you stay for any length of time in a hotel it is a good idea to give a 'mid-way' tip to the waiter and chambermaid. 20,000 lire per week each is about right in a medium-range hotel.

Cultural institutions

American Academy (*Accademia Americana*), 5 Via Angelo Masina, 00153 Roma, tel. 581 8653
British Council: Palazzo del Drago, 20 Via Quattro Fontane, 00184 Roma, tel. 475 6641
British School at Rome (*Accademia Britannica*), Piazza Winston S. Churchill (61 Via Gramsci), 00197 Roma, tel. 87 3424 or 87 0513
Keats-Shelley Memorial House, 26 Piazza di Spagna, tel. 678 4235
American and English Bookshop, 181 Via del Babuino
American Bookshop, 57 Via della Vite
Economy Book Center, 29 Piazza di Spagna

Useful telephone numbers

Emergency: 113
Directory Enquiries: 12
Traffic conditions (Rome): 194
Weather forecast: 1911
Taxis: 117, 8433, 86 9398, 3570
Alarm-call service: 114
Telegrams: 186

Important addresses
Diplomatic offices

British Embassy
80a Via XX Settembre
00187 Roma; tel. 4 755 441, 4 755 551

United States Embassy
119a Via Vittorio Veneto
00187 Roma; tel. 4 674

Australian Embassy
215 Via Alessandria
00198 Roma; tel. 832 721

Canadian Embassy
27 Via G. B. de Rossi
00161 Roma; tel. 841 341

Irish Embassy
3 Largo del Nazareno
00187 Roma; tel. 6 782 541

New Zealand Embassy
28 Via Zara
00198 Roma; tel. 4 402 928

Tourist information offices

In UK
Italian State Tourist Office (ENIT)
1 Princes Street
London W1R 8AY;
tel. 071 408 1254

In United States
Italian State Tourist Office
630 Fifth Avenue, Suite 1565
New York, NY 10111;
tel. 212/245 4822–24

In Rome
Ente Nazionale Italiano per il Turismo
2 Via Marghera;
tel. 497 1282
(also at Fiumicino airport)

RAC
RAC Motoring Services Ltd
RAC House
PO Box 100
South Croydon CR2 6XW;
tel. 081 686 2525

Trajan's Column

Useful words and phrases

Although English is often understood in the parts of Italy frequented by tourists, the visitor will undoubtedly find a few words and phrases of Italian very useful.

please	per favore	town hall	municipio
thank you (very much)	(molte) grazie	exchange office	ufficio di cambio
yes/no	si/no	police station	posto di polizia
excuse me	scusi (I beg your pardon), con permesso (when passing in front of someone)	public telephone	telefono pubblico
		tourist information office	ufficio turistico
		doctor	medico
		chemist's	farmacia
do you speak English?	parla inglese?	toilet	gabinetto
I do not understand	non capisco	ladies	signore
good morning	buon giorno	gentlemen	signori
good evening	buona sera	engaged	occupato
goodbye	arrivederci	free	libero
how much?	quanto?	entrance	entrata
I should like	vorrei avere	exit	uscita
a room with a private bath	una camera con bagno		
the bill, please (in restaurant)	cameriere, il conto!	today/tomorrow	oggi/domani
everything included	tutto compreso	Sunday/Monday	domenica/lunedì
when?	quando?	Tuesday/Wednesday	martedì/mercoledì
open	aperto	Thursday/Friday	giovedì/venerdì
shut	chiuso	Saturday/holiday	sabato/giorno festivo

where is .... street?	dov'è la via ...?	0 zero	8 otto
the road to ...?	la strada per ...?	1 uno, una, un, un'	9 nove
how far is it to...?	quanto è distante ...?	2 due	10 dieci
to the left/right	a sinistra/a destra	3 tre	11 undici
straight on	sempre diritto	4 quattro	12 dodici
post office	ufficio postale	5 cinque	20 venti
railway station	stazione	6 sei	50 cinquanta
		7 sette	100 cento

Index

Original German text: Toni Kienlechner. Translation: R. Gordon
Series editor, English edition: Jane Rolph

© Verlag Robert Pfützner GmbH, München. Original German edition

© Jarrold Publishing, Norwich, Great Britain 1/91. English language edition worldwide

Published in the US and Canada by Hunter Publishing, Inc.,
300 Raritan Center Parkway, Edison NJ 08818

Illustrations: A. Boardman pages 1, 3, 12, 22, 23, 44, 64, 66, 87; J. Allan Cash Ltd pages 19, 35, 37, 55, 83; B. Clark pages 9, 86; James Davis Travel Photography page 69; D. F. Goodrick page 52; R. Gordon pages 21, 49, 74; D. Halford page 53; Italian State Tourist Office (E.N.I.T.) pages 29, 73; I. Roll page 17; H. Thompson/N. Jeans pages 30, 31, 40, 43, 88; Travel Trade Photography page 93; World Pictures Ltd cover and pages 46, 47, 48, 51, 63, 68; J. Young pages 32, 89.

The publishers have made every endeavour to ensure the accuracy of this publication but can accept no responsibility for any errors or omissions. They would, however, appreciate notification of any inaccuracies to correct future editions.

Printed in Italy

ISBN 0–7117–0480–5